Also by the Author

The Great Crowd: A Love Story about a Large Urban Parish

To Make Myself a Word: The Collected Poems and Images of a Parish Priest

ON GIVING MY WORD

Poems, Stories, and Aphorism of a Priest in Retirement

MICHAEL J. TAN CRETI

 iUniverse®

ON GIVING MY WORD
POEMS, STORIES, AND APHORISM OF A PRIEST IN RETIREMENT

iUniverse books may be ordered through booksellers or by contacting:

iUniverse
1663 Liberty Drive
Bloomington, IN 47403
www.iuniverse.com
844-349-9409

Because of the dynamic nature of the Internet, any web addresses or links contained in this book may have changed since publication and may no longer be valid. The views expressed in this work are solely those of the author and do not necessarily reflect the views of the publisher, and the publisher hereby disclaims any responsibility for them.

Any people depicted in stock imagery provided by Getty Images are models, and such images are being used for illustrative purposes only. Certain stock imagery © Getty Images.

Cover art by the hand of Jane F. Tan Creti, in the tradition of the Prospon School of Iconology.

ISBN: 978-1-6632-4679-0 (sc)
ISBN: 978-1-6632-4680-6 (hc)
ISBN: 978-1-6632-4678-3 (e)

Library of Congress Control Number: 2022919062

Print information available on the last page.

iUniverse rev. date: 11/15/2022

CONTENTS

Fragments of a National Narrative

Fragments of the Spiritual Narrative

Fragments in Text

Fragments of Flesh

The After Story and a Return to the Text

The End of the Narrative: Resurrection

INTRODUCTION

In 2010, I published a collection of poems and stories that had accumulated during my twenty-nine years of ministry at All Saints Episcopal Church, in Omaha, Nebraska. In many ways, the pieces composed a sidebar to my ministry, a kind of conversation with myself and my God. In retrospect, I saw in the words of these poems and stories the beginning of a translation of myself into a single word, a self-expression, that would ultimately represent the essence of who I am. It occurred to me that publishing them would be valuable for me and possibly for others as an encouragement for my and their continued efforts at self-expression. The result was *To Make Myself a Word: The Collected Poems and Images of a Parish Priest.*

Shortly after that, I was asked to write a history of All Saints, which I was reluctant to do. I rather understood my retirement as a freedom from having to explain the parish and the Episcopal Church to the world. I trusted that this freedom would allow me to turn to other forms of writing that had always taken a back seat in respect to the practical demands of pastoral life. The pressure to do so, however, continued, and I finally relented, with the proviso that if I did, it would not be a typical parish history that chronicled the succession of rectors, building projects, and the so-called great events. It would be an attempt to narrate the way an American parish had responded to its social context and navigated the changing currents of theology through the course of its 120-some years of existence.

What emerged from four years of research and writing was a narrative that I came to understand as a love story. It was published in 2014 under the title *The Great Crowd: A Love Story about a Large Urban Parish.*

As was true for my ministry, this occupation did not preclude a sidebar of poems, stories, and formulations, the latter of which I came to think of as aphorisms. This collection has continued to grow in the course of the past five years. As I look back on them, they now seem ripe for publication as a new collection held together around the idea of narrative. The function of narrative was nurtured not only by my writing a parish history but also by the cultural shift that has taken place in the beginning years of the twenty-first century. While 9/11 is a significant marker of this change, the change was much more complex, as is evident in way that it has affected the whole Western world, and from the impact that it has had on the living experience of religious communities.

Left behind were the generous trends of the twentieth century's final decades: ecumenism in the sphere of religion, civility in the sphere of the state, and willingness to take risks in the sphere of the individual. In their place came a renewed confessionalism, a political correctness, and a guarded self-interest. The politicization of communities at all levels has meant the loss of story, which has been progressively replaced by positions. This means that communities have been transformed into parties and individuals into partisans.

This was reflected in a shift in my own sources of inspiration. In the early collection, I indicated that my inspiration came largely from the metaphysical poets of the seventeenth century, particularly John Donne, George Herbert, Henry Vaughan, and Thomas Traherne. In radically changed religious and cultural institutions, they were able to find a means of inhabiting an experience of the transcendent God. This mysticism allowed them to affirm their subjectivity, their own "I," that the exterior world threatened to define for them. At that time, I very much needed that affirmation.

In my retirement, my need was altered, and I found myself drawn to the works of S. T. Coleridge, and to those who were most indebted to him, F. D. Maurice, J. H. Newman, and James Marsh. They, in the nineteenth century, were living through a crisis much like our own. This crisis was about the "we" and whether or not one could hold on to it. I recognize that it is not only the culture but the stage of my life that makes the "we" problematic. If you doubt that, wait till you retire!

Coleridge's influence is most obvious in the use I have made of aphorisms. In 1825, Coleridge published *Aids to Reflection*, which throughout the nineteenth century remained a must-read for individuals of the Anglo-American world interested in spirituality. It was a collection of aphorisms with extended commentary.

An aphorism is a concise formulation of thought meant to be unloaded by means of a thinking process or, perhaps better yet, a meditative process. I found myself thinking through a number of knotty problems, many of which remain unsolved but some of which have been resolved into an aphorism. I have used these accruing aphorisms as a kind of skeleton on which to hang the poems and stories that resulted from a parallel imagination process.

The poems and stories are arranged in six narratives: original, natural, personal, national, spiritual, and final. It is my sense that there could be a great number of narratives undertaken between an original and a final narrative—the most obvious one would be, dear reader, your own. In this collection, the spiritual narrative is the Judeo-Christian narrative, which I recognize is not necessarily everyone's, but it is clearly mine. It is my intention in the fragments of the spiritual narrative to free the narrative from doctrinal limitations, which at their worst intend to preempt the narrative. It may be that, with some exploration, my reader might find this narrative theirs as well. What is clear is that all narratives under the sun are parts of a single narrative that often escapes our notice, but not us, as a matter of fact!

Even in our own personal narratives, we must confess that what we offer are only fragments that await completion from a time and source other than our own. Between the origin and final end, all narratives are in the process of revision. I am only too aware that what I offer with this collection is a very limited and very temporary work, whose hope is that the reader might get a sense of their own participation in the formation of narrative.

It is my own belief that the two tracks, aphorism and literary units, complement each other, save for my own ineptitude in either genre. Nevertheless, I have printed the aphorisms in italics, which will easily allow the imaginative reader to pass over them and the thinking reader, to a somewhat lesser extent, to pass over the poems. This, of course, misses the point that a very central part of our present cultural crisis is the disassociation of thinking and imagining. Be that as it may, the spirit of this collection is *giving*, and a giver has no right to specify how a gift is to be received. Make what you can of these words, and in turn, give back what you can with words of your own.

Michael J. Tan Creti
Edgerton House, 2020

Postscript: Two and a half years have passed since the writing of the preceding introduction, but it seems right to retain it, since the residency in Edgerton House and my time on the Dartmouth campus during the fall semester of 2019 allowed me to put the material together in a coherent whole, and in retrospect, it identifies very well what this book is about. In part this delay is due to the COVID-19 pandemic. We returned to our home in Omaha, my wife with a unique icon for Kountze Commons and I with my book, only to find ourselves spending our fifty-third anniversary on a COVID-19 honeymoon. It was not all a loss, for there are some additions to the text from the pandemic experience and several rereadings that have enriched the text—the last of which I have just finished, and I found the text still provocative. It is a pleasure at last to send it on to you.

Michael J. Tan Creti
Home in Omaha, 2022

With Gratitude
For the Prospon School of Iconology
Vladislav Andrejev,
Founder, Iconographer and Theologian
Olga Andrejev,
His wife, Hostess, and Principal Coordinator
Jane F. Tan Creti,
My wife, iconographer and principal muse
For the light
In
the face.

THE ORIGINS OF NARRATIVE

THE ANGEL OF GOD'S SILENCE

How is it that we know of your silence,
if it were not from some messenger,
some dark angel, who has come in the night
and revealed it to us?

APHORISM §1 SILENCE

―――◈―――

Silence is not what frightens me, for silence betokens presence. It is the buzz, the music of futility, that terrifies me.

THE WEAVER'S WHISPER

―――◈―――

I heard the silent weaver whisper an ancient word,
one from before the dawn of time,
as her hand was guiding thread
across a growing web.

APHORISM §2 SILENCE AND TIME

⸻◈⸻

The knowledge of time is held in the silence of God.

*"It is not for you to know the times or periods
that the Father has set by his own authority" (Acts 1:7).*

THE ICON OF THE DESCENT OF THE HOLY SPIRIT

⸻◈⸻

In the icon of the descent of the Holy Spirit,
often there is depicted a strange little man,
wizened and crowned,
in a cave beneath the upper room
where the apostles are gathered to pray.
He presides over twelve scrolls laid out on a cloth.
Some say he is Father Time,
Chronos himself,
but that seems strange, unless
time is bound up with the procession,
as light is with the begetting.

APHORISM §3 THE ENIGMA OF TIME

Time is an enigma that has scarcely been addressed in human thought. Among the ancients, the most notable exception is Augustine of Hippo. His lengthy discussion of time in his Confessions *was without precedent, apparently prompted by the collision of ancient philosophy and biblical chronology, to which he was determined to give equal justice. Augustine's ideas were considered authoritative by many for a very long time, but his essay on time was largely ignored. Among the moderns, we might note the curious case of Heidegger. He was an heir to a phenomenology that was very much time bound, and he promised in his foundational work* Sein und Zeit *to do justice to time, which philosophy had up to then avoided. He did not, however, keep that promise, either because it was beyond his ability to do so or, worse, because of his corruption. His heir apparent Jean-Paul Sartre interpreted his work, perhaps correctly, in* L'Être et le néant, *which seems to equate time and nothingness. It is true that time is nothing to a self in relationship to things. It is only something of importance when the self is in relationship with another. Time, in that context, must be reckoned with.*

Consciousness of time is something distinctly human. When we leave our dog at home, my wife tells our dog that we will be back in five minutes, since she is convinced that five minutes and five hours are the same for a dog. If the dog has ever caught on, she has not mentioned it.

The consciousness of time begins with the memory of a past to which one cannot return, the only return to the past being memory. In time, memory makes clear that a now is distinct from the past. Further recollection will at some point make it clear that the present now will become the past of another now. Thus arises the problem of time, past, present, and future. Locating ourselves in such a flux is daunting. To do so, we must summon our profoundest virtues: faith, hope, and charity. It is by being faithful to the past, hopeful about the future, and charitable toward the present that we can find wholeness.

FAITH, HOPE, AND LOVE

Faith remembers the past.
Love embraces the present.
Hope yearns for the future.
Yet faith has no plan to return to the past.
Faith hopes to make a gift of it to the future.
Love has no plan to hold on to the present.
Love hopes to send its beloved to the future.
Hope has no plan to replace the past or the present.
Hope keeps faith with the past and loves the present.
Indeed, love being faithful, faith being loving, and hope being both
make it clear that the three are one trinitarily.

To have found time in our consciousness is an imperfect answer, open to the charge that time is, then, a subjective reality and has no objective foundation in reality. Is time, then, really nothingness? The closest that we come in a rational explanation of time is to identify it as a dimension, the so-called fourth dimension. But that metaphor of dimension is precisely the source of the enigma, for unlike other dimensions, it travels in only one direction. One cannot travel back in time!

Unless one is willing to enter into a transcendental and/or mystical interpretation, one must accept that a very large piece of our experience remains outside our grasp.

On the one side of a mystical inquiry is the troubling perception that the divine otherness is in some kind of permanent withdrawal—some kind of stepping back.

On the other side of a mystical inquiry is the equally troubling perception that the divine otherness is in some kind of permanent advance—some kind of stepping out.

Transcendental analysis, however, maintains that such polarity is precisely what we would expect to find at the foundation of reality. Translated into theological language, these polarities are an Eternal Father begetting an Eternal Son by stepping back, an Eternal Son honoring His Eternal Father by stepping out.

In this language system, the polarities are resolved by a third kind of movement. Simultaneous to stepping back, the Spirit proceeds from the Father to the Son with a loving endorsement: "You are my Son, in whom I am well pleased." And simultaneous to the stepping out, the Spirit returns from the Son with the loving acknowledgment "I love to do your will." Thus, the Eternal Spirit is the back-and-forth movement (shuttle) that becomes the divine context of Eternal Time.

THE QUIET WEAVER

Chance,
accident,
human machinations,
politics both enlightened and crass
rule, rock, wreck, and wrench but never sway your church,
for the weaver ever works new thread across an ancient warp,
adding colors, bringing forth patterns rewoven from below,
new woven from above, and mixed kaleidoscopically,
at which future generations will marvel and judge,
but which we ourselves will never see or more than guess.

Oh, quiet weaver, self-effacing and hid,
from where have you come, and whither do you go?
And where is it that you have learned this craft?
But in the depth of God, from where you do proceed,
for the movement of love toward a begotten one
and again returned to a begetter
is the art of the shuttlecock
to make whole cloth.
God's act,
purpose,
plan.

This may seem to be mythic language, and more than the secular thinker is capable of accepting. Yet mythic language is inherently timeless. The theological language that I have employed in the preceding text is time-full. *This language system is not mythic, because it is grounded in narrative and therefore wedded to time.*

For some time, secular science was content to be timeless. When it began in the nineteenth century to direct its thinking to dynamic aspects of nature, a small letter t *made its way into its formulas. This was a largely neutral concept, until Einstein took it into the field of relativity.*

The secular mind, if it wishes, can explore them by means of other terminology, but not to do so is to leave a very large chunk of reality unthought.

APHORISM §6 THE TRAJECTORY OF CREATED TIME

Created time is a trajectory that originates from the central value of the Spirit, the midway between stepping back of the Father, into which the past is drawn and hence is inaccessible, and the stepping out of the Son, from which the Future is summoned and hence is unattainable, until all is in all.

Created time begins, then, as a bubble at the midpoint of the Spirit movement, where initially it is no more than a nutshell—that is, immensely small. For a moment, it is held in tension between the stepping back and the stepping out. It is divided into matter that will be drawn back into the past and into an inspiration that will be drawn on into a future. It is succeeded by a bubble, perhaps better identified as a wafer, ever so much bigger, containing a line of memory and a line of aspiration. Thus, created time is a line marked by a sequence of ever-increasing wafer-like bubbles. Presently, I should think that the bubble is approximately thirteen billion light-years across—still, I suspect, small in terms of what is to follow.

If this leaves much unanswered about time, it provides an open framework that allows further exploration by means of a narrative, whether by scientists or humanists!

MEDITATIONS ON THE CONSCIOUSNESS OF TIME
Prompted by the Thoughts of Edmund Husserl
See *Essential Husserl*, "Consciousness of Internal Time," p. 205

1

"The tone now sounds, and it immediately sinks into the past."

A note has sounded and called me to a present now.
It has resonated with a past struck tone held in my memory.
It has moved in me an expectation of yet more notes
and the possibility of a melody not yet heard.

Because of that note,
I have entered in the stream of time,
leaving behind the timeless night,
which is not the place of love
but the place where memory and expectation
are exchanged for a self in its self.
Love rides the stream,
sharing memories,
daring dreams,
allowing the self
to be dissolved
and yet resolved
in the narrative
of another's making.

2

Clearly there is no consciousness of time
until there is a memory of a past
that once was now but is not now.
The now in which I am is known
because I have a memory of a past now,

and once I am aware of this, this now
must realize that it is already sinking into the past,
making room, as it were, for a new now.
So it should be clear
that memory of a past that once was a now
is the source of the expectation
and consequently the intuition of a future.

3

"To that extent, the intuition belonging to expectation is memorial intuition
turned upside down, for in memory's case the intentions aimed at the now
do not 'precede' the event but follow after it."

To remember you, O Lord, is to expect you.
A lover of wisdom once said
that the intuition belonging to expectation
is the same intuition that belongs to memory
turned upside down—
together they define the conscious mind.

So I should think that intuition begins
with the first instance of memory.
You, Lord, are my first memory
and my last expectation,
the model of every memory,
the template of all expectation.

4

This I remember:
a now that is past.
The now that I know presently
carries something of that past in it
and is already on its way to anticipating another.

Through them run a movement that carries forward
as if they stood on a hidden landscape
that is time itself.

Space-time is not an emptiness
but a plenum
through which things move,
propelled, as it were, by a hidden field.
Light is bent by the space pocketed by gravity.
Life is restrained from running backward
by the downward decline of time, drawn by eternity.

YOUR WORD

Your Word, long ago, came to me in a secret place.
Sometime later, I found it again in the narrative
of a little church, clothed, as it were, in Carpenter Gothic
and peopled by the minions of the main street
of a small, decidedly prosaic, mid-America town.

Since then, I have pursued it down
through the course of a century that burned itself out
not in the ultimate tragedy with which it continually flirted
but in the embrace of a banality to which it unabashedly yielded.

CAN FLESH BECOME WORD?

If Your Word became flesh,
could it be that my flesh can become Word?

And if it did, could it run down
the verso side of the universe,
with a million million other words,
caught up in an eternal narrative?

But how could that be?
Unless You were to speak to me!

Why should I dare to think that,
save for a memory that I once heard You call—
"Michael, become the word I am seeking"?

Why would you be seeking a word—
indeed, why would you need me to be that word—
unless you were in the midst
of telling some really great story,
some vast romance, scarcely begun,
that could take an eternity in its telling?

LEGACY

Legacy is quicksilver,
comedic and lethal,
smoke in the wind,
wax before fire,
rain on a river.

So if, and to the extent,
I became a word,
not to explain
but to claim
the "I"
in an unselfed me,
and if then I could let it pass
as a word into another's narrative,

wouldn't that be sweet water
on the tip of my Lazarus's finger
to suffice me
for the long last journey
down the face of God
before the final fall
into eternity?

REMEMBERED

The thought that one might be remembered,
or, as likely, disremembered,
for whatever time that might be,
is little more than a decoration on a grave.
But for some word of his to still be at play
in someone else's mind—
that would border on eternal life.

AN OLD MAN

An old man sat silent at the end of the hall,
and it occurred to me that he had a story to tell.
I sat down next to him, and he shared his name.
So a story began.

FRAGMENTS OF A
NATURAL NARRATIVE

APHORISM §7 A DIFFICULT MISTRESS

Science is always a difficult mistress for Theology. The Old Science, who has been lingering on her deathbed for the past fifty years, presented Theology with a universe of solid particles bound in an implacable order that has existed long before humanity appeared on the scene and would be there long after it disappeared, not a little relieved by its passing. The New Science, who is, at first blush, both charming and elegant, presents us with a universe of fields all dependent on a base field named Higgs, after the man who imagined it. If it were turned off, the universe would dissolve in a blink of an eye or perhaps run backward and be turned inside out.

SOME MIMSY

1
Ode to the Quantum Moon

My eye tonight has caught the Quantum Moon
high in the midnight sky.

And glad I am to see it there.
I have been told it's there because it's seen,
so I willingly add the field of my own frail and fleeting look
to all those myriads of others, including that of the sun,
which holds it there.

Still, it has a special relish for me—
that it is not entirely beyond quantum jitteriness
and that in some depth of its being it might be hoping for a blink
that would allow it to step out into a nowhere,
and then to appear elsewhere,
and then, in cultivated nonchalance,
return to just being there.

Ah, Quantum Moon, let that be for us our secret tie.

2
The Paired Particle

Once, in night school,
I sat at the feet of a wizened paired particle,
who asked me in the gravest of tones
how it could be, given the classic rule
that information from point A, which was he,
could travel to point B, which was his pair,
even if in nothing less than a wink in time,
and over nothing less than a bite of space,
that he was not unpaired by now?
Which, he had to confess, he wasn't.

Troubled, I replied, "Sir, you know."
Careful I was to avoid his eye,
and after a pause, he instructed me
in a weighty voice:
"The time-space that lies between point A
and point B is not the only way.
At each point is a back door
that opens onto the all-at-once,
onto the order of the risen again.
Which is why we will not be unpaired!"

APHORISM §8 THE ERROR OF THE CREATIONIST

The error of creationists is that they forget or deny that the creation stories, the biblical one as well as others, presuppose a given science. Moreover, the intention of a creation story is other than prescribing science from continuing to develop.

The error of scientists is that they forget or deny that their science is based on presuppositions that, if they are not, certainly look like theological propositions. Moreover, the intention of science is not to prescribe theological developments, and, indeed, it often finds itself mystified when an ethical response to its findings is not forthcoming.

CUPPING

Cupping, that subtle curve
that rules all evolution,
begins with a wafer of matter
and a parcel of information.

THE ULTIMATE SHOW

I dreamed that I had visited the land of ultimate smallness
and that there I had been convinced to go
to a magician's act that was billed
the Ultimate Show.

THE JOURNEY OF THE MIND TO
ULTIMATE SMALLNESS AND BACK

An Invitation

My mind feels bidden to go
to the place of ultimate smallness,
to the spring from which all existence flows,
and from there to retrace that starlit path
along which the becoming immensity grows,
in which is lodged what we call the self.

I don't intend to be gone long—
I'll only pause to sweep
away some fallen leaves
and to watch the water clear.
You, too, should come, my dear.

To the Spring

The way is not so direct,
but made by a multiple number of slicing and dicing
until divisibility becomes an impossibility,
because the object no longer has a place or a time
and since the apparent solidity of things
has dissolved into strings,
into waves of energy constantly moving,
ever eluding any attempt to determining
their precise position or dissipation,
bringing to my mind the metaphor
of the dawning new day.

"Morning has broken like the first morning.
Blackbird has spoken like the first bird."

The first word spoken is apparently a constant,
a number not so big as to suppress progress,
causing it to fall back on itself,
nor so small as to allow progress to disperse,
causing it to lose itself in terminal variance,
and not in either case to annihilate the possibility of a self.
At the first event
(inaccurately styled *the big bang*),
that which is now so immensely huge
was so incredibly pinched,
so that it is nearly adjacent to the time,
we would find in a visit to the ultimately small.

There, the dimension of time shrinks
for those like ourselves who would visit it—
in a way, that is like what one would experience
in that moment that followed the first event.

The First Cup

Stepping back ever so little from the ultimate smallness,
one sees the strings threading into space-time,
leaving behind moments of indeterminacy
and spinning into existence
up, down, strange, charm, bottom, and top particles
before returning to their hidden realms of indeterminacy.

The array of particles clump,
forming disklike structures
that appear to be quite determined,
except on their edges,
where one might notice
a particle suddenly deviates,
falling into or out of the disk.

How this can be,
since there appears to be
no force to move the particle,
escapes an answer,
unless indeterminacy lingers in the string
by which it was generated.

Even more inexplicable is
noting its return to the place left behind,
as if somehow it remembered where it had been.
Which is utterly impossible,
since memory requires information,
by which it could recover its past and return to it.
Information, say, that was exchanged
between itself and its opposite number
on the other edge of the disk.

But there is no place or form
for such information to exist
in and/or between two inert things
separated by space,
empty or filled with other things—
at least not in the regime of three-dimensional space.

But the string that brought
a trace of indeterminacy into that space
might lead a line of information out of that space into dimensions
filled with transmissions of electromagnetic radiations
that bend that which appears to be straight,
in much the same way as light is bent by gravitation,
yielding hollows that fill with information,
albeit the thinnest imaginable line of code—
"I am here; you are there," which is hardly profound,
except for the implication of a relationship
that is, when it registers,

so mind-bending.
One cries out, "My God!"
except for the restraint
of a fear that it might preempt
the process of inquiry
on the journey back
before it had hardly begun.

On some golden pond,
quieted and shaded
from the sting of ultraviolet rays—
or was it in the spewed midst,
rich with minerals of some thermal vent,
or in some conjoining of the two,
that a film of fatty acids clumped,
balled, and then spread into a double layer,
held long enough to fold and bend
in the primal pattern of cupping,
until water was both without and within?

Was this life or the edge of life?
Whatever. By it, the earth was changed.

APHORISM §9 THE TORAH IN THINGS

The Torah is in things from the very beginning, and it surfaces in time in a text. Of course, the text is not Torah but the appearance or face of Torah, though this text one is invited into the knowledge of Torah—or shall we say into the Light, in all things.

Has it not been said by the psalmist, "One day tells its tale to another, and one night imparts knowledge to another. Although they have no words or language, and their voices are not heard" (Psalm 19:2–3)?

APHORISM §10 THE SOUL OF THE TORAH

When Rabbi Kook spoke to his students about the soul of Torah, he was referring not to a Platonic Essence, as one might be tempted to think, but surely to a Hebraic Nephish. Torah at its creation is infused with breath. It is living, not dead.

APHORISM §11 THE UNIVERSE AND NARRATIVE

The universe is the subject of a narrative, not simply an object in one.

Discussion of the biblical account of the Creation has focused largely on the first three words of the text, which are translated as "in the beginning," or on those verbal acts such as the commandments in the pattern of "Let there be light." Yet the most important text for understanding this account, "These are the generations of the heaven and the earth," is largely passed over with a smile, as if this was some kind of simplistic gloss. The book of Genesis is, in many ways, a genealogy that is making the point that the story of generations is our story as well, making us children of Adam, Eve, Abraham, and Sarah. This verse insists that the coming into being of the heavens and the earth is a story in itself and that its story is our story as well.

Strangely, scientists are commonly thought of as undoing, and sometimes themselves think that they are undoing, the Creation story. But consciously or not, they are in fact doing it. The crucial issue of a Creation account is not the how but the relation that exists between it and us.

APHORISM §12 THE ODDITY OF THE HUMAN BRAIN

The so-called oddity of the human brain strikes me as a misnomer. It is similar to looking down the evolutionary scale and calling the presence of bacteria in our world an oddity.

When I look back, it seems to me that the human brain is a response to the lines of information present in the earliest forms of matter who reside in the realm of quantum physics.

When I look forward, it seems progressively clearer that the human brain involves processes that reprise quantum physics. If that is the case, it seems even more obvious that "oddity" misnames it. In that case, it might arguably be said that it is something close to the telos of everything.

If that is not so, would it make sense that there is in our experience a long-standing, ubiquitous attempt to tell the story of everything?

APHORISM §13 BRAIN AND MEMORY

———◆———

A headline announces "Amoebas: They May Not Have Brains, but They Have Memory." In the story that follows, we are told that amoebas have been shown to be able to remember the way to food even after the food stimulus has been removed for as long as ninety minutes. The explanation is that a thread of information is embedded in the amoeba that dissipates over time. This should not be surprising since patterns of information occur in inanimate reality and can be remembered in a way that restores a former state.

This can be viewed as an advance on inherent potential of reality. It is not, however, properly styled as memory without a brain, and even the evolution of a brain will not suffice to transform remembering lines of information into memory. In order to be memory, there has to be information about information, an order that emerges only in the highest levels of consciousness.

THE MEANING OF A LINE

A hundred thousand years ago, in the land of Lingjing,
a human shade passed a piece of bone
drying in the sun and stooped to pick it up.
Its broad flat surface caught his eye
and triggered a thought that it might be soft to touch.

A shattered rib of a fallen beast,
about the size of his lower arm,
which he deemed to be of no small worth
and pondered long what to make of it.

But he found himself unable to decide,
often letting his finger glide
across its broad flat face,
thinking that it must be a special place.

"For what?" he would ask himself,
until the day he passed the quarry
where he with the others pounded flint
and left flakes fall, which could cut.

Carefully fetching one
with enough heft to hold,
and yet edge that one would not dare to touch,
he returned home and sat down with the bone.

He hardly dared to let the flake touch the bone,
but on the fourth or fifth pass, he saw that it left a trail
across the face that had filled him with such awe.
Now he could not dare to repeating that stroke.

Restraint prevailed, but his restless hand wanted more.
So he moved a measure up the bone and let it go.
He saw now that the first trail was not an accident,
so he repeated it a third, fourth, fifth, and only a minor sixth.

It was done, he realized, and knew that he had seen
what in nature could not be seen: a line.
He hid it from others for fear that they would think him unnatural.
He hid it from himself for fear that he would think himself mad.

Till he began to think that the line had been a sign
of a higher way of seeing and deserved to be hallowed
in the common way of his people, dressed in ocher red.
So he left it dressed and re-etched, for the world to find
a hundred thousand years afterward in the land of Lingjing.

APHORISM §14 HOMO SAPIENS AND HUMAN BEINGS

Homo sapiens *are a fact; human beings are an aspiration. If the latter ever exists as a fact, it would be, I think, on the same order as a Higgs boson, which exists as a fact for ten-sextillionths of a second. Still if the analogy holds, the weight of the universe somehow depends on them.*

A HAND

A hand in red was
left on the wall of an ancient cave,
in ocher earth, which the same hand had spread
about the face of the dead
tucked fetal-wise in a shallow grave.

It was not left
for us to discover,
but for the other for whom darkness is light,
the one for whom day is the same as night.
It was a red prayer.
Which moves me
to want to kiss the earth
and become part of that red prayer
for those who now rest in its care,
for I yearn with them for the promised birth.

FRAGMENTS OF A PERSONAL NARRATIVE

APHORISM §15 PERSONAL STORIES AND THE NARRATIVE

Narrative begins with the personal story, and from there, it can take on a number of forms. The personal story can transmute itself in the story of a fictional hero or heroine, or it can embed itself in a social history. All these alternatives disguise the fact that the root of the narrative is one's own story. "I was" is where it necessarily begins.

These alternatives are prompted by the fact that a personal story will appear to be egotistical, as if telling it meant that it is more important than someone else's story. No one's story is more important than another's. The bottom line, however, is that one's own story is the only story that one has to tell. It is important that the telling presents itself as an invitation for others to tell their stories. No story is complete in itself. Each story requires the stories of others to complete it. It is from the body of stories that the great narrative takes off.

I walked through the halls of the Joslyn Art Museum in Omaha, Nebraska, in the summer 2018 and was taken by a new acquisition, which lead to this fragment that belongs in my personal narrative.

THREE WOMEN IN THE AIR
Hayv Kahraman, *Mnemonic Artifact 3*, Joslyn Art Museum
(Image is available online.)

At the end of the marble hall, I stop and think,
Who are these women tumbling in a mouse-gray space?
    I am looking for some tether to retrieve them,
            some umbilical cord to feed them,
                some lines to distinguish them,
                    some gravity to bring them down.
But no. There are none to be found.

Which leaves me wondering where to begin
    with these three women, who are much too alike.
    The one on the lower right seems to cast a shadow of gold—
        Arabic tiles, I think.
    On the lower left, she seems cupped by some blue—
        a run of water, perhaps?
    While the one in between, the one up in the air, has none.
Then it dawns on me the three are one.

They are the artist's mother moving though gray space and ash like time,
    and she is trying to remember her,
        her severed past, her present habit, her future hope.
    See where the canvas has been cut by the artist's own hands,
        across a breast, a brow, and hands that reach and almost touch,
        driven by some kind of commitment to the way it was.
        Then the artist has taken linen bands and with those same hands,
        as if to stanch the wounds,
            woven them across the cuts in a likeness
    to the palm fans of her lost childhood land.

To a life unmembered, she is saying, "I will remember.
          I will remember as long as I can make art."

Why now am I remembering my mother,
          as if she, too, moved through gray space and ash like time
                    and tumbled through some strange arc,
                    from Little Lucy Locket at the dinner table
                    in the large wood-framed house at the bottom
                    of the hill where the town turned to string
                    and families spoke German to one another;

                    to the blond Lucky Strikes girl,
                    claimed by the dark Italian boy passing through
                              her farm town, wracked by depression,
                              and poised on the brink of world war;

                    to the widowed mentor of her daughter,
                    navigating the "me" decade of the American seventies,
                    rejecting that atomistic individualism
                    that had allowed her own strange adventure.

          It's hard, I must confess, to see that she was one
                    and that I, too, am somehow the child of a migrant mom,
                    uneasy about the way I belong to this here and now,
                    except by remembering through the artifacts of my own making,
                    woven through the cuts and clutter of my life.

Now as I move on, making way for you to stand, here, where I am,
          I take solace in my thought that you, too, will be moved to remember—
                    to remember your own becoming, and that, much like me and her,
                    you, too, are migrants,
                    migrants all.

Kodak photograph taken by my parents of themselves
on the lawn behind her parents' house, 1939.

THE BRIDGE

The imprint of the Mormon Bridge is etched in my mind
        from many crossing under its green towers
        over the obscure ford used in their westward flight.
My native state lies on the east side of the bridge,
        the state of my vocation on the west.

Many times, I have traversed this bridge
        on the way back to my childhood home
        and again upon my return
        to the home of my laboring,
        parenting, and likely my dying.
The bridge is the locus of mysterious feelings.
        On the way back home, it is the place
        where the mental occupation of my vocation yields
        to dealing with the unfinished pieces of my childhood.
        And on the way forth, it is the point
        where the mental work of my occupation returns
        to the yet unstarted pieces of my future.

It is strange that a bridge could give rise to such feelings.
    The deep swift Missouri beneath it
    that separates two lands
    represents an inner separation
    as deep and as swift,
    as treacherous and forbidding—
    no more so, I think—
    that holds apart my birth and my vocation.
A life is cut by so many such rivers
    that it might seem that there is never any returning,
    that every passage is to a greater and greater isolation.
    But the crosses in the bridge's scaffolding point contrarily—
    Christ is the bridge that never lets separation be the final truth.

DESIRE, IOWA

In a dream, I was buying ammunition,
rifle shells, a thing that I have never done,
trying to discern the meaning of carefully drawn
circles and lines on the packages, which, as close as I could see,
must have been equal to the hole they would make on passing through.

The salesclerk asked me where I was from,
and hastily I responded, "Iowa."
Realizing that this response was wrong or at least misleading,
I backpedaled to avert any untoward consequences
and explained, that is, from the Iowa that is west of the Missouri,
not Carter Lake, which was separated from Iowa
by the flood of 1877.
The hole had gotten deeper, when in a sudden flash
I appear to have found the saving formula,
from "Desire, Iowa," that is.

AN ODE TO A LITTLE CHURCH

⚊⚬◆⚬⚊

I

Finding God

When I found you, it was in a little wooden church,
Carpenter Gothic, as they say, not without a touch of irony,
        built on the crest of the nineteenth century's optimism,
                1885, to be exact,
        only to be shuttered during the trough that followed,
                when optimism soured
            and then broke in the next century,
    and then unshuttered by a wave of postwar enthusiasm,
                1952, to be exact.

This reopening coincided with a strange set of family circumstances
        that brought me to the catechetical efforts of a newly ordained priest,
        the Reverend Charles Bradshaw, the sincere, if clumsy, scion
        of a prominent family of Des Moines, the capital city of our state,
        well placed among its lawyers and bankers.

    This and the presence in the congregation of a district judge
    provided my father in spite of his religious inclinations,
            he was after all the son of an anticlerical father
            and a pious Catholic mother,
            a common pattern of Italian immigrants,
    to consent, after twelve years of marriage,
    to his wife and his children attending this little church.

    My mother, for whom this little church was equally strange,
    found in its strangeness a kind of self-assertion,
    amid her general pattern of acquisition.
    How clearly I see her at the confirmation,
    which followed the season of catechism,
    receiving the same laying on of hands as I.
    Regal, I would say—it was only later,
            when a college classmate visiting in our home
            remarked, to my surprise, that she was beautiful,
            that I, for the first time in my life, so saw her.

In the summer of 1956, I, with my younger brothers,
   painted that little church,
            then reopened for a total of four years,
            but still looking in many ways shuttered.
   It followed the summer before,
            when we had begun mowing the churchyard,
            my father ashamed of the uncut grass
            and doubly motivated by his vision of his own WPA
            by which he could keep his kids engaged in manual labor,
            good, he was sure, for ensuring our manhood.

Up to then, our painting expertise was constrained
to the endless repainting of the wooden fence that surrounded our home.
How we managed to move that wooden extension ladder,
secure but weighty, I cannot imagine,
nor, in the end, what sort of result we managed to achieve,
beyond the whiteness running down from the eaves.

In my father's eyes, this made the little church littler.
In mine, I almost said, grand,
but the truth is that I never could see it
without looking through my father's eyes,
so, I would say to my hands,
            it made the little church feel more concrete,
and the encounter with its clumsy catechetic,
            and with its odd collection of humanity,
            more real.

Indeed, at the time, I remember thinking
that its very woundedness made it possible
for me to put my hand into its side,
and with that, I could cry out, with Thomas,
"My Lord and God."

II

Ordained a Priest

I was ordained your priest in a little church
      that sat on the north end of Clear Lake, Iowa,
      on the twenty-second of December.

The day was marked by an arctic cold,
which had followed the previous day's snow,
deep and drifting, enough to made travel all but impossible.

Once a chapel for a summer camp
on the other end of the lake,
the structure had been moved across the lake on the ice
when the camp was closed in favor
of a larger, more centrally located camp.
There it was christened St. Andrew's.

As one might suspect,
its picturesque trusses
held up an uninsulated roof
anchored to rustic walls and windows
that anticipated an endless summer
but not the arctic cold of this day.

The new foundation had been laid in the optimism
that had warmed the country at the end of the war,
increasing its faith, faith even in our little church,
which was soon to be broken anew
on the brittle faults of American life,
from successive shocks.
In the no less cold of the following January,
the Tet Offensive cleaved American public opinion,
opening a gaping wound
that wouldn't be closed for years to come.
In the long-anticipated April,
as I was preparing for my first Easter mass,
Martin Luther King was slain
on the landing of a motel in Nashville.
The nation was halted in it tracks
by the need to bring some kind of sanity to its life,
as was our little town, which had no persons of color
but which harbored that year the fear that hundreds of blacks
would arrive on buses from Chicago to picket its lakefront.

Still, when that little eclectic congregation gathered for that Easter,
it was as if new fire had come up from those very foundations.

III
Made a Priest

When I arrive at my first church,
    I was struck by what a strange pool of people they were,
    certainly not the congregation I had imagined in my formation.
    It was difficult to fathom what held them together,
    why they came back, as they did, in their own indiscernible pattern,
    or what they believed or what they expected.
    I could have easily dismissed them,
    but some grace allowed me to see that it was to them I had been sent
    and that it was to them that I had been called to give myself,
    trusting in the mystery of who we could be.

    It was they, more than the formal formation,
    more than ordination itself,
    that made my priesthood,
    and they have, in fact, never left it.

IV
Sent

Following my second Christmas mass, the bishop moved me
    to yet another little church for which he had more hope or need.
    I was never sure which, and maybe he wasn't either.
    The church from which he removed me
    ceased to exist a few years later.
    The new church was less rustic
    but just as modest,
    a Quonset hut, remarkably disguised,
    an ugly duckling, to be sure,
    but graced with a gracious and learned congregation.

    How our conversations would soar
    in the issues of theology and social discourse,
    community development and/or cultural change.
    We were players.

    I finished in that little church flush with hope
    and went back to school to argue the case of my little church

in the great halls of the larger church
in the cavernous priory of St. Rose of Lima,
with the Dominicans, Franciscans, and Norbertines,
          nestled high above the river that made Iowa's east boundary.

V
The Quest for the Great Crowd

Completing three years of graduate study
          made it time to find a job to relieve the sacrifice
          that my family had been making, three kids now in school,
          and my wife, who nursed on the hospital's evening shift.
          Finding one proved harder than one might think.
          My bishop, it occurred to me, was suspicious of what I had become,
          and seemed to point me away from any ready solution.

Then by chance a church outside my diocese
          struggling with a largeness that required an assistant,
          but was having a comparably hard time finding someone
          who could see themselves as someone's assistant,
          called me.
          My family and I were transported across my Iowa
          to Omaha, beyond the river, on its other side.
          In truth, the rector and I were an odd couple,
          being of distinctly different temperaments and talents.
          It was only supposed to last for five years
          while I completed my dissertation.
          Yet we worked well together,
          which the congregation found amazing,
          inspiring them, I think, to work well with each other.
          There were indeed some great crowds,
          many initiatives, and a congregation hungry for more.

When it came down to a final edit of my dissertation
          to the satisfy peculiarities of my committee—
          remember that back then everything was typed by hand,
          entailing no small cost and no little time—
          I found that I was, by then,
                    so into living theology in a congregation,
                    and writing it on human hearts,

that I did not have the heart to do what was required
in order to qualify for living theology in academia,
and doing theology in classes so transient,
and in books so problematic, largely unread.
I left the editorial work undone and went on.

Went on in that congregation until twenty-nine years had gone by
and the quest for the great crowd
had, by then, turned into a love story.

A CONFESSION BEFORE THE HOLY ANGELS

"I confess to God Almighty, to the blessed Mary ever virgin,
to the blessed Michael the Archangel. . ."
Compline of the Diurnal

Before the regard of God, I confess
to Michael my vulnerability,
to Gabriel my ignorance,
to Raphael my unwholeness,
to Uriel my incompleteness,
to Sariel my fear of dying,
to Remiel my lack of mercy,
to Raguel my failure as a friend.
Wherefore I beg you, holy angels,
pray for me to the Lord our God.

A CONFESSION OF A RECOVERING MISOGYNIST

I lie beside my wife of forty-nine years,
waking in the morning hour
when the dark has just broken
but the light has not yet come.
My hand holds her knee,
and the thought passes through my head
that I should somehow confess to her
that I was a misogynist.

I am puzzled by this thought
and have no clear idea of why it has entered my head.

A dream that dissolved upon waking, perhaps?
There is, in fact, little evidence on record
on which an indictment on this charge might rest,
me being a processor
who has left so much unsaid
and who has rather over the years
carefully censored what he did say.
That means that the evidence that could be produced
would be, at best, circumstantial.

So why has this conceit jumped out of the box
and not dissolved in the light?

YOU SHOULD KNOW

⟫⟩◆⟨⟪

I am, in fact, a recovering misogynist
raised in the fifties, in small-town Iowa,
which means I was steeped in it.
My father, whose terse comments on women
can be reduced to one that I recall:
"They want to get their hooks in you."
Which probably explains, in part, why I never dated.

The other part of this was, I suppose,
my mother's pain at my father's anger,
which frequently flared out in spite of their love for each other,
and his relentless demands that everything be just so.

I left home to attend an all-male college in the East,
after which I spent two years in the navy on an all-male ship of the line,
and then I went to an all-male seminary in order to enter an all-male profession,
harboring in my mind a vision of a life in an all-male order.

It is no wonder that at that point I had no clue.
Save once I remember in a course on European history
running across the name of Rosa Luxemburg,
that turn-of-the-century Polish Lithuanian Socialist,
and thinking, *There is a woman with whom I could fall in love!*

As I have said, I never dated—
that is, until the summer of my first year at seminary,
when I asked a young woman I had met out to dinner,
in retrospect a safe structure of a first date.

I did fall in love with that first date,
but still I had no clue,
as all misogynists make exceptions
for a mother, a sister, or the matriarch
(given that in small churches women are the majority),
or for their lover.

I date my sobriety to 1969, the year I came to Grinnell,
that strangely liberal college on the plains
in that sober rustic Iowa town,
both drug infused and shaken by radical protest,
by antiwar demonstrations, and by a rising tide of feminism.
There I encountered exceptional women:

Dr. Betty McKibben, professor of classics, a Latinist,
noted as a teacher too ready to give what she knew to others,
threatening the economy of higher education.
She was the heart of the small church to which I had come to serve.

Jane Sellers, the epitome of a gracious housewife,
a joyful member of that same small church but connected
with the upper echelons of the college hierarchy through her husband
and passionately committed to day care for working women.

Sally More, the wife of a professor of English literature,
a slender southern belle dressed in charm,
gloved with lace covering a fist of steel,
a strident feminist, and a passionate environmentalist.

Julia Sears, a brilliant student, headed for law school,
the feminine center and the practical head of hip Grinnell's
one true commune, located in a dilapidated farmstead east of town,
and yet with her husband, Phil, in our small church every Sunday.

From them I learned, and with them I made common cause.
        Floyd Beaver, the town mayor, was known to have grumbled,
        "What are Tan Creti and the women up to now?"

From them I knew for the first time what I was,
        and I set out to change that,
        always aware how easy one could fall back into it.

I find it strange that this storm of remembrance floods my mind
that might just as well have been forgotten,
were it not for the present crescendo of misogynism in American life.
How shall I explain to them that fifty years later
I am losing sleep because of this vision of recidivism?

THINKING IS FUN

In the predawn light, I had awoken,
turned to a different position in my bed
to relieve a pain that visited in the night
to gnaw on my hip,
and I promptly had fallen back into a leaden sleep,
the kind that is worried by dreams.
When I awoke a second time, I remembered the words:
"If one could think, it still would be fun."

It was advice given in the wake of a crude surgery
that had involved the removal of a leg
precisely at that point of a hip
that was like the one that had previously awakened me,
but it is unclear to whom it was given.
For in part, I was the practitioner of this barbaric art,
but in the end, it seemed as if somehow
it was I who was in the pain
and it would be I who was left without a limb.

Thinking is fun,
not, of course, calculation,
which is a lonely art
stalked by the angels of the dark,
by pride and fear.
I suppose it is because
the purpose of calculation
is for the other to become an object.

In its first flush,
rising over the other, it becomes a pride,
but then in the fall,
sinking under the other, it becomes a fear,

of not loving the other as the self.
And, worse, that God himself
has been made an object of calculation,
alas, an idol.
What fear?
What pride?
No love in that.

But thinking, as I have said, is fun,
for when I am thinking, I am not lonely.
It is done in the company of angels
and in the presence of God.
It is a response to others,
casting out fear,
embracing humility,
falling in love,
causing objects to become the others,
and I—I to become someone else's other.

Indeed, the art of thinking
fulfills the second law of the universe,
the first as well.
Alas, the holy other,
what trust,
what joy,
what love,
what utter fun!

CONVERSATIONS WITH NONAGENARIANS

1

Estelle

A Tribute to Estelle Faire on Her Ninetieth Birthday, February 3, 2017

When I think of past conversations with Estelle,
      I am reminded of moments
      when they evoke in my imagination
      the image of a determined Brooklyn gal,
      a faithful and demure daughter of Israel,
      descending a dark flight of stairs into the underground
      where the Eighth Avenue Express
      barrels its way toward the Fulton Street station.
It is, I should think, late summer in 1945.
      She is dressed neatly in the fashion of the time,
      in a carefully ironed, primly buttoned blouse
      over one of those great circle skirts,
      shod with saddle shoes
      and white bobby socks expertly rolled.

      She boards the train quickly,
      and thanks (she smiles to herself)
      to her diminutive stature,
      she has achieved near invisibility,
      and, once seated, utter abstraction,
      which together are the secrets
      of successful riders of underground trains.
What music or art inhabits her mind on that day,
      who can say? Perhaps it is the falling notes of the appassionato,
      the rising mirage of a maiden suspended in a Chagall sky,
      or hid away in a sunlit corner of a William Merritt Chase story,
      any or all of which would have lasted till the telltale shudder

when the express crosses Broadway.
There with her fellow riders
she would have poured through the doors
and joined in the race to the place where the uptown boards,
after which she would have settled back
into that invisible abstraction
until the stop at Morningside Heights.
There she, at a deliberate pace, would have ascended into the light
and crossed through a campus, only to climb again stairs.
This time up into a venerable building and through it
to a classroom of students, mostly males,
who consider these halls of science and math
to be their special domain.
They would have looked quizzically
at this diminutive Brooklyn girl
in a way that quite clearly asked, "What are you doing here?"
And she looks back, not yielding an inch,
"You'll find out when they hand out the grades!"
All that would explain why years later
she could see herself in the celebrated photo
of a black girl neatly dressed in a circle skirt and bobby socks
walking at the front of the nine, into Little Rock High,
and why zeal, justice, truth, and compassion
have so often resonated
in those wonderful conversations with Estelle.

2

A Special Pair

Morley was the ultimate sentimentalist.
He felt things deeply, did things enthusiastically—
he relished fellowship hardily.
His religious sentiments ran deep as well,
though he often struggled with moving from feeling to practice,

which led him to question his faith.
Why the same prayers every Sunday?
Surely that was nothing more than religion by rote?

Erickson was the ultimate rationalist.
He reasoned about things rigorously, did things thoughtfully,
and he was always up for a good argument.
His religious thinking was voracious as well,
though he had difficulty in accepting doctrine,
which made him question his faith.
How can you speak a language that cannot be verified?
Isn't that the definition of self-deception?

It occurred to me that the conversation with the two
was like sitting in on an exchange of those French philosophes
Rousseau and Voltaire,
the former of whom loved religion but hated the church
and the latter of whom valued the church but hated religion.

Morley for all his dark ruminations
never let them stand in the way of his fellowship.
Erickson for all his critical thoughts
never let them separate him from a rite well done.

I would often tell them that in the end
they were not so very different,
for feeling arises from faith,
even as thinking begins with faith.
Faith fails only when one stops feeling or thinking—
they never did.

THE END OF FAITHFULNESS:
COMEDY, TRAGEDY, OR GRACE?

Early I vowed faithfulness
and held it between me and my God
until it was claimed in part by Jane.

In the noon of my days,
when my libido ran full flood,
it was my pride that somehow
it held with that Jane too.

But in the back of my mind,
there lurked a fear
that somehow with time
my pride would break
and my libido would carry me off
to the comic fate of a mocked and hampered Falstaff.
Or else my libido would break,
and left to my pride, I would rail against my offspring
and come to the tragic fate of a reviled and outcast Lear.

Now on the edge of the dark,
it would appear that by some stroke of luck
both broke on the same day,
and in my end, I am left with faithfulness
and pondering the conundrum
that my life has accomplished
neither great comedy
nor high tragedy—
indeed, nothing
more than grace,
thank God.

IN THE MOOD TO HOLD ON

The sun itself has slipped beneath the horizon in the west.
Still, it sends its light high up on the tops of trees
that tower over my head,
where it paints autumnal gold and red
on limbs chilled and bared.
And I am in the mood to hold
on as long as it is there,
and I think that by doing so
I am shortening the coming dark
that will separate this moment
from when it will rise red in the east.

NASTURTIUMS IN FALL

Late a mound of Nasturtiums has come,
a cache of yellowish-green pads held on slender stems,
beneath which lurk deep yellows, reds, and oranges,
bashful blooms the colors of the sun.

Just in time, it would seem, before the first frost,
which hovers in these nights and will fall some dawn,
turning the pads dark green and baring the slender stems,
revealing their now gone blooms.

I have a mind to scold them for wasting the summer,
which they judged too hot for doing their best.
Better, I think, to scold myself if I don't pick a bouquet
from beneath the pads and bring them in for us to see.

Better to thank them for saving their show
till when other blooming things are worn and dry,
a feast of color for the eye before the coming snow.

WALKING THE STATIONS OF THE CROSS BACKWARD

On a winter's walk, I followed the dog
     down the steep hill behind our house,
     relishing the crunch of the snow in the dry sunlit air.
     I found myself in the bottom, where the stations end,
     and whimsy suggested that I walk up their path
     to the top, where they began.
     It would be a good sequel to the stomp, I thought,
     that had brought me down.
     Then it dawned on me that
     I would be beginning with the vindication of the fifteenth
     and would be walking backward to the corrupt judgment of the first.
     I pondered for a moment what harm would come
     from such an ahistorical approach.
     I soon, however, began to realize that the images of suffering pointed
     not just to the past but very much to the present as well.
     I was not simply playing history backward,
     but it was exploring the fact that the resurrection had led
     to a history of suffering, one that had not yet slackened,
     which raised the question that when I came to the corrupt judgment,
     whose judgment that would be—
     Pilate's or denizens of all the corruption judgments
     that come down to our present world,
     even those of the very church
     who had claimed the resurrection as its ground?
It appears that chance in league with a dog had taught me that day
     a better understanding of the complexity of that way.

A SHORT JANE SONG

When Dante encounters Beatrice
in the thirtieth canto of the *Purgatorio*,
he inquired how she was,
to which she replied, "We are fine."

Already with you, my dear,
I have begun to be that "we."

TO MY BELOVED

Our legacy shall be word for me and light for you.

LIGHT ON THE WORD

Largely, it might be said,
the medium of artists is light,
an appeal to the eye.
The geste of poets is word,
which is meant to be heard.

Still, upon reflection
it might further be said
poets by setting words on paper
want to be seen.
And artists by means of keeping silence
want to speak.

Whether this trespasses,
the one on the other or not,
cannot be fairly judged without remembering
that in the beginning was the Word,
who was also the Light of the World.

LET US GO OFF

Yes, yes, let us go off to sleep
in some distant wildly deep
under some other sun,
far from the race we've run.

A DARK WOOD

I am left pondering what has turned this on
after a dormant spell that seemed
by mutual consent the way it would be.
Is it something we have left behind
or something we sense to be ahead
that this has come back to our bed?

A CURIOUS FACT

I have told my reader once before
that my beloved's desires peak in the morning
while mine have always belonged to the night,
so it will not surprise you that upon an early awakening,
I was mulling in my mind a curious fact—
that the family of fauna had developed a gut
long before it had developed a heart.

After a second or third time around the block,
I became aware of a fire growing at my side,
to which my own fire began to rise, more, I confess,
in my imagination than in my flesh,
but, however, lacking at present,
it was flush from the past.

When it had run its course and cooled,
she slept at my side, and I returned to the thought
and wondered if that meant that gut feeling
had some kind of priority over heart felt.
And it occurred to me that
if I lost my beloved,
perhaps my heart would throb,
but, for certain, my gut would wrench
and wring from me a most awful sob.

A LATE JANE SONG

At a time in the night
that was not exactly clear,
after the usual nocturnal urination,
but well before the thermostat dutiful
prompted the warming of the house
for our morning rising,
we became mutually aware of the other
being awake and so moved closer,
and her body, like the young woman
she once was, invited more,
though, if I remember right,
back then, it was I that was doing the inviting
and she the consenting.

But for some time now, that has been different—
why or when that became so
I do not pretend to know—
and she sent me down,
deeper, to taste her,
and I thought,
somewhat surprised at my age,
We are making love,
but then I never like that phrase,
and rethought,
Love is making us.

THE PRIEST IN AN OPERA OF GRACE

He sings to the mirror of his ideal self.
It is ill defined and subject to change,
it having come to him from his father,
not without an element of misogyny,
and comically it mocks him.

He sings to the woman who loves him.
In her he sees his real self,
evermore defined and lined
with the passage of time,
and she gracefully humbles him.

APHORISM §16 SEX WITHOUT A NARRATIVE

There is a scene that regularly plays in modern romances. A man and a woman are suddenly alone and start a frantic removal of each other's clothes, at least enough of it, so that penetration is possible, always in the most awkward of positions. It seems as if someone is holding a stopwatch whom they must somehow impress or else be disqualified. But circumstances seldom seem to suggest that this is the case or that there are other issues that require this speed. That causes me to think that the real reason is that this haste precludes the need for a narrative. But what is sexual intercourse without a narrative?

ON FINDING A BREATH PRAYER

———⋖◇⋗———

Since the first time I read Salinger's *Franny and Zooey*,
    the year it was published, if my recall is accurate,
    I considered my inability to find a breath prayer
    for my spiritual life to be its glaring error,
    due, one had to conclude, to a lack of will.
    My attempts to accept my limitations and move on
    were periodically troubled by the reoccurrence of its claim,
    such as the fashionable devotion in the seventies
    to the mantras of the East
    and then to its counter from the West,
    the centering prayer of Spencer Abbey,
    and on to my growing interests in Eastern Orthodoxy
    and its well-known Jesus prayer,
    but to no good end.
So it was with utter surprise that late in my life,
    wakening in the middle of a deep night,
    I heard myself say,
        "Lord, I am not worthy that you should come under my roof,
        but speak the word only, and my soul shall be healed."
    I smiled and asked myself,
        "What communion do you suppose you are about to receive,
        here, as it were, on your bed in the middle of the night?"
I breathed it in and out a time or two
    and fell back into a needed sleep,
    avoiding somehow that barren wakefulness
    that has so often robbed me of sleep's gift.
Later that night, I did the same,
    and now it fills the spaces of night,
    day, as well,
    making my coming end,
    whether in the day or night,
    an act of communion.

APHORISM §17 THE PROBLEM WITH COMMUNION

Communion is problematic. Some would say that it is impossible—for example, existentialists—and no one should be under the illusion that it is easy to come by. In order to find it, we can begin by considering the nature of experience. The self experiences the other in three different venues: in things, in human beings, and in divine transcendence. This experience of the other in respect to things and human beings is referred to as intuition, in respect to divine transcendence, mysticism. In any case, it is the nature of experience to be episodic, incomprehensible, and ineffable. This would appear to be the end of the story were it not that the self possesses the faculty of memory. An experience is remembered in various degrees, which gives rise to the recollection that at a certain time and/or a certain place, I had an experience. Thus, the self begins telling a story to the self, which produces an interior dialogue. It is a small step to sharing this story with God and even, with some effort, with another human being. Communion begins!

IN SEARCH OF THE EDGE

I have come here in search of the edge,
to this modest chapel, at noonday,
not unlike the horde of others who pursue the edge.
It is, after all, inherent in being us.

Except those others, for the most part,
seek it up and out there
in the distant reaches of time and space
only to find more of the same,
except progressively attenuated
and ever more determined.

Here I am focusing down and in—
in the closeness of my soul,
where things get infinitely small,
become edgy
and ever more indeterminate.

Where I am free
and able, not necessitated,
to choose or not choose,
which is the only way I can be faithful
to what I did choose: to search for the edge.

UPON THE SETTING OF THE TABLE

O Bread of the Earth, I would follow you
      through prayer to the depth of your making.
O Word from Above, I would wait for you
      rising in the bread to the moment of breaking.
O Weak Flesh that I am, I would move you
      in haste to the place of my taking.
O Soul within Me, I would prepare you
      with longing for the day of your waking.

WHEN IN THE UPPER ROOM

When in the upper room
Jesus laid hands on the bread,
what was it that lay in his grasp?
A crust? A slice? A loaf?
Meant for a passing moment?
Or was it more?
I have heard poets say that his hand
laid hold of the miller and the baker as well,
of the sower and the reaper,
all together being blessed and broken.

So now I wonder
if I might hear a scientist say that his grasp
held on to it down to its ultimate smallness,
back to its emergence from the original singularity
and all the becoming of 13.8 billion years past.
And if that could be said,

I should think that this bread
placed on my lips,
being unrestricted by location
and salted with indeterminacy,
would burn like the coal placed
on Isaiah's lips.

Then I should not doubt
that the bread of heaven
was also the bread in my throat,
that the bread of freedom
was also the bread in my alimentation,
and that by it my life was being made new.

COMMUNION IN THE PANDEMIC OF 2020

I am puzzled by all the talk focused on communion abstinence. It strikes me that this reduces the Eucharist to a means by which the institution makes communion available, when, in reality, Eucharist defines Christian life. I live Eucharist every day, every hour, as best I can. Daily, I attempt to gather myself in a way that I can offer it to God. I say, "Lord, take me." "Lord, bless me." "Lord, brake me." "So, Lord, I might be communion for someone."

I profoundly miss weekly Eucharist, indeed midweek Eucharist, because it models the pattern of my life. Even there, I am not so intent on consuming and being consumed.

So the discussion ought to be about how the Eucharistic action of church life continues under the severe straits of the pandemic.

RAMBLINGS OF A VERY OLD PRIEST

In the third month of what we now call the COVID-19 pandemic,
we were given a sign of what was to come
as we were instructed at a funeral mass
that the rule was sip, don't dip.
The humorous mnemonic apparently envisioned
that the prohibition of intinction would suffice,
which is now best forgotten
save as a reminder of how unprepared we were
to deal with what was to come about.

Scarcely into Lent, when our church counsels a physical fasts
as a means to a spiritual end, our state ordered a spiritual fast

as a means to a physical end, prohibiting public worship,
something that I have had difficulty getting my head around.

I can, of course, see the value of the physical end
of not being infected is a necessary good,
not to avoid dying—I am well past that preoccupation—
but in not having to be cared for,
and/or infecting those others around me.

Still, I was struggling to see the good in the spiritual fast
until one night in the course of this fast I had a dream.
In the dream, I was feeling strangely hungry,
which had me pondering what had brought this on,
until I noticed how my hands reached out,
which made it clear that it was for that bread
that is given only by he who is risen from the dead.

As hunger from a physical fast makes bread taste sweeter,
so I am thinking that a spiritual hunger will make his bread dearer.

HOLY WEEK IN THE PANDEMIC

The prospect of Holy Week without Eucharist seemed most harsh. It was difficult to imagine it without that action by which our Lord's death is shown until he comes again. When Maundy Thursday came, I was intent to hold a virtual Eucharist and pondered as I did if I should not choose to wash some virtual feet. The thought occurred to me that if I should play the Lord, I should like the feet to be of one from Wuhan, some brother or sister, a widower, an orphan, or some survivor.

When the bread of life lies broken
      on the cold stone table,
      the Spirit hovers o'er it.
      Its order lies in chaos
      till it is lifted
      and we are fed.

Then, with the breath of life within us,
      in our fevered frame,
      it seeks the waters
      locked within its rock
      till it is freed
      and we are quenched.

Now the fount of life lies beneath us
      in its originating silence,
      enveloping both the Spirit and the Word
      till it envelopes us
      and we are in communion.

I WILL DIE IN A SMALL CHURCH

It is now clear that I will die in a small church.
I had once thought that it might be in some great church.
I wrote in a diary, when I was seventeen,
five years after discovering God in a small church,

"I am not satisfied by it, or any other form of religious establishment."

I can't say that I know what the boy was thinking when he wrote that.
I do know that later he had aspirations for a great church which,
        after serving for seven years
        as the vicar of two small churches,
        both of whom he loved deeply,
        and even now recalls fondly:
        Hap Connally, Dutch Schultz,
        Bill and Betty McKibben,
        Al Pinder, Dorothy Palmer—
        I mean, he could pretty much name them all,
        and sometimes finds himself doing so
        when he wakes in the night,
    led him to the Dominican Study House in the great priory
    of Saint Rose of Lima on the bank of the Mississippi
    not far from where Julian Dubuque made his landing.
The priory was a large foundation of the fifties which never
        fulfilled the grandeur it imagined for itself.
        When he arrived, it was seeking an alternative grandeur
        by offering, with the Lutherans of Wartburg
        and the Calvinists of the Dubuque Seminary,
        degrees in ecumenical theology,
        envisioning a truly great church.

He was sure that there he was writing a theology
>for his little church that would be so embracing
>that it could be ignored by only the most intransigent,
>drawing it into some greater church.

He imagined that he would die in communion with Rome,
>at peace with Geneva, and in agreement with Concordia.
>But in the pressures of the eighties,
>ecumenism was sacrificed
>on the altar of political expediency.
>Church leadership responded to the crisis in their communities
>not with a call for faith, apparently not remembering
>their Lord's promise to be with the two or the three,
>but trusting the invincible politics of fear and guilt
>which promised to provide a fierce hold on people
>and a ready explanation for any who dared disaffection.
>So that great church never happened.

On leaving studies, he went to work in a large urban parish
>that aspired to assemble a great crowd.
>With them, he practiced ecumenism and lived theology,
>and experienced some great crowds, or so it seemed.

But now that ecumenism is gone, so, too, is the great crowd.

So as the night comes, he, that is, I,
>am resigned to dying in a small church,
>now free from the distinction of great and small,
>and I have no doubt that in a small church God will find me.

GIVEN LIFE, IN RETROSPECT

I have given my life to a small oddity in Christianity,
the Episcopal Church in the United States of America.
In the midst of its current troubles, I want very much for it to succeed.
Still, I would say this commitment is, and never was, without a sense
that through it I was doing something for the greater body of Christians,
be they followers of a pope in eternal Rome,
of Pentecostals in the forests of Brazil,
or of evangelicals in an emerging China.
I want very much for this body to grow, yet with all of that,
I would not want it to become the world, but in this world
to be that humanity that the spirit calls it to be.

OUT THROUGH THE GARDEN

———◆———

"Honey," I said, "I'm going out through the garden."
    She misses the humor in my remark,
    or, more likely,
    she has chosen to ignore it.

To me she is a little too much of the world
    that doesn't keep track of the score.
    Once, it was common to speak of the score,
    as in three score and ten, or four score and seven,
    but now, to speak of a score is either comic or contrived.
    Somewhere along the line, the score has disappeared.
    I suppose it was when the mechanics took over keeping the time,
    and as a result, we have become experts on minutes and seconds
    but no longer seem to know the score.

With that unspoken thought, I am out the door,
    intent on losing myself in the garden,
    and think as I go, I should at least say to her,
    "You could come too."

A BRIEF HISTORY OF GARDENS

The first garden was Eden, which was planted by God.
>It was, of course, perfect, except it appears to have been a little viny,
>for Milton alleged that Eve on that fateful day went off by herself
>to arrange those profligate vines and thereby incurred in her head
>that buzz that apparently said you can know the difference
>between good and evil ever much as God himself.

Adam's garden was filled with weeds,
>and its fruits were garnered in by the sweat of his brow.
>Daily he coaxed from its earth the bread of life,
>and daily the earth whispered back to him, "I'll bury you."
>He did not doubt that it would
>but for all of that loved it nonetheless.

There followed in time *The Garden of Earthly Delights*,
>painted by Hieronymus Bosch with unparalleled insight.
>Lushly fruited and with contrivances never before or since seen,
>centered on a lucid watering hole,
>around which parade a plethora of fauna
>and dance a multitude of males and females,
>splayed about in extravagant mirth,
>all of which is hinged between
>a pristine time before
>and a very dark time after.

Voltaire's garden was an idea in his mind,
>which he commended to all: "il faut cultiver notre jardin."
>By Jefferson, it was made into a virtual laboratory,
>testing 330 kinds of vegetables and 170 varieties of fruits,
>all meticulously noting for yield, over against time and circumstance,
>and assiduously cared for by tireless Wormley Hughes,
>Jefferson's man slave.

My father's garden was driven,
>one might say, from leftover fear
>from gardening on the Vermont subsistence farm,
>where he was raised in poverty with nine siblings.
>It was overplanted with potatoes, tomatoes, and beans

in order to stock a root cellar and fill jars put up by my mother
and tidily shelved in our basement, never fully consumed.
The tending of it fell to us children and was accompanied with lectures:
"The Irish poor in Boston had rickets.
The even poorer Italians had none
because they grew and ate green peppers."
His garden was out of proportion to our progressive entrance
in middle-class life, but as with the green peppers, it was to remind us
that in regard to middle-class life, we were to remain outliers.

In this oversize garden, which often got the best of us, as gardens do,
there was a plot, six by six feet, if I remember it right,
that was *my garden* that I could plant as I liked as a kind of dissent,
and I suppose that is why through a number of moves and changes in my life
that garden continued to grow in my own backyard.

My garden in all its permutations is filled with memories.
When I mulch my asparagus,
I remember my German grandmother,
whose asparagus bed lay just outside the chick pen.
I am still trying to equal it and think my disadvantage
lies with the lack of a hen.
When my spade turns earth, I remember my Italian grandmother,
who at eighty rebelled against being confined to a "kitchen garden"
by spading her own.
When I plant green peppers, I remember my father's lectures
on how the poor Italians didn't have rickets.
When I pick gooseberries, I remember my mother's anguish
at debearding each one for such a modest sour return.
When I weed my beans, I remember my little brother,
lying down in the row in order to watch them grow.
In fact, my garden is a book in which my life can be read.

Christ's garden was called Gethsemane.
Its most precious fruit were the drops of his blood
that fell from his most sacred brow.
Is this, then, the last garden
in which we will sow
before the tow
takes us down and out?

I SLEPT IN THE GARDEN

I slept in the garden,
and when they led you past, I looked away.
Now, lying under the cross on a bed of rock,
I should like to taste the flaming air
drawn down into your drowning lungs,
made large by your feet pushing against the nails
and by the pull of your arms on the crossbar above,
lasting no more than a fleeting second,
a draft begun with relish
and half drunk before falling into the dark.

A FREE ME?

A determined wave is driving me
onto a foreign shore.
The hour and the means are not sure,
but no less inevitable than the fall of a tree.

It would make me no more free
to know the when and how of its coming.
The only thought worth troubling
is what in a foreign land the free me could be.

TOSSED ON THE FAR SHORE OF ETERNITY

I was born where the dirt is black and sweet
and the hills roll in gentle folds before a steady eye,
and it is in them that my youthful formations lie.

But like some Israelite, I went down to sea in ships
and was troubled and tossed about
and in due time was cast up and out.

In the end, I went back to the dirt that is black and sweet
and the hills that roll in gentle folds before the eye,
and it is there, it now appears, that I shall die.

But I am glad for having gone down to the sea in ships,
for in the end, it seems to me,
we shall all be put out to sea.

So I think I am better prepared to go down to eternity,
and no matter how black or troubled that sea
and no matter how lost and staggered I be,

I shall be glad to have known both the dirt and the sea,
for having received my life from the one
and gained my legs from the other.

And when I am taken and tossed by a sudden wave
bent on bearing me to that distant shore of eternity,
I shall call them all sweet, sweet dirt, sweet sea.

AFTER LIFE?

Dreary and disappointing are the images of an afterlife.

First wrought by the minds of ancients who committed their dead
to dark underground haunts, filled with shadowy forms,
or ersatz castles built in the air, shared with demanding gods,
made palatable by the waters of forgetting, drunk from the yellow
Lethe,
or bought off with concocted gifts made by descendants seeking
relief.

Hardly transformed by the medieval enterprise,
quantified and merchandised by clerics,
painted and sculpted by temple artists,
embellished and celebrated by court poets,
all of whom trusted that fear would their ignorance disguise.

Allegedly dispelled by the dawning of modern lights
who claimed that they had the courage to just call it dark.
But not so entirely convincing as to keep their children
from sprinkling their mother's ashes on the eighth tee
or equipping their father's tomb with his tackle box.

Are there, then, no images of afterlife that are transforming and merry?

APHORISM §18 LIFE AFTER DEATH

Contemporary talk about life after death is vague, incoherent, and easily rejected because it consists largely of content borrowed from the past. The failure to revitalize it is due to a number of causes, not least of which, to my thinking, is sheer laziness. Even Christianity in its viral youth allowed the ancient concepts of soul, underworld, and denizens of the deep to front for its more revolutionary ideas of body, soul, and resurrection. This compromise has persisted through three revolutions in the human understanding of reality.

A program of reform would require three steps. The first step is to reject the legitimacy of the term afterlife. *Second is to use a modern sense of reality to identify where life that exists in space-time could find an alternative existence. Third is, on the same basis, to reimagine the nature of body-soul.*

1. The expression afterlife *implies that one's life is somehow separated into two lives: one that takes place in space-time and another life that follows death in an alternative domain. On the one hand, this is an invitation for fantasy, and on the other hand, for ridicule. Less obvious, but perhaps of greater concern, the term "afterlife" fails to properly value what is at stake in this present life, reducing it to an irrelevance. The proper term is "*life after death.*" As such, it is able to identify the essential matter involved in the living of this life which continues to live on after death.*

2. The challenge of a continued existence outside space-time is often referred to as the dismantling of a three-storied universe. The life after death was never simply tied to the concept of a three-storied universe, but it was an easy way to win arguments! Instinctively, very early humans sought transcendence in the netherworld of caves, as is evidenced in the stunning prehistoric cave art. Transcendence did not come from the cave, but the cave became an effective metaphor for it. In time, instinct was transformed into myth, and given the grasp of reality at the time, it made sense. But with the rise of the science of modernity, it became progressively less convincing, and in its ascendancy, modern classical physics has declared it an impossibility. In our own times, the impact of quantum mechanics and information science has begun a serious reorientation of our sense of reality. The nonlocality principle in quantum mechanics has been resisted not by the religion establishment, as were the former advances in science, but by the scientific establishment itself. This advance suggests openings for transcendence, which has long been in question because of life in the box of space-time and because of the rigid sense of the location of things. Those who begrudged what quantum mechanics had implied about reality would insist that there is some boundary after which the quantum effect no longer is in effect. But that is entirely arbitrary. Quantum effects must still resonate in large and complex bodies, even if they remain elusive. It is true that their effect is submerged in the large and complex levels of reality, but it is not clear that under some circumstances it could reemerge, making way for a life that is not here or there to continue as a life.

3. The association of life with a body implies that life cannot exist without a body. There can be, accordingly, no life after death since the body returns to the earth, dust to dust, ashes to ashes. Long before the Judeo-Christian ideas of life after death, the idea of the immortal soul attempted to get around this objection. This was problematic because the ability of imagining the life of a soul was never anything more than a fantasized version of corporal existence. The Judeo-Christian insistence of a body-soul that was distinct from flesh and blood never fit easily with the concept of an immortal soul. Nevertheless, it was simpler to ignore that dissonance as believers apparently fell in line.

What is clear is that a physiological definition of a body was never an adequate description of the reality indicated by the term body. *There is an underlying structure to a body that distinguishes it from things. That explains why the construct of an immortal soul was attractive even though there was no evidence for one. However, with the new information science, we have a means of identifying what makes a body special. We can begin by identifying in the simplest ultrasmall particle a line of information. When we rise to the largeness and complexity of the human body, we recognize that in it and under it is a vast collection of information.*

The beauty of a person is not in the visual form, as in idealized Greek marbles, but it is in the posture or presentation, due to the way information holds the body up and out! The life-after-death problem on this level is simply the question of whether or not this information, which is the essence of the body, is preserved. Whether it is or is not comes down to faith, which should be no problem since life after death shouldn't be anything less than an issue of faith. What is significant is that, in this way, the question can no longer be dismisses as unreal.

The reformation of life-after-death language will not be easily achieved. Nevertheless, the crisis grows, and both the rants and the platitudes are wearing thin. The judgment of the world looms, and we have nothing to say to the world or to the dying unless we can bring this off. This sketch of such a reform presents a very preliminary guide for such a reform.

FRAGMENTS OF A
NATIONAL NARRATIVE

AMERICANA

The American Dream

———◆———

Be forewarned.
>   The American dream is not a narrative,
>   or else one could date and place its birth,
>   could speak of the home in which was raised
>   and of all the changes it had made along the way,
>   but in the end, there is nothing more to say,
>   which prompts one to ask if it is indeed a citizen.

ON THE PRAISE OF A PARTICULAR STAR

———◆———

My learned friend, be not so quick
>   to call that Puritan poet sin-sick
>   who confessed that he was unable to make a noble song
>   to praise the morning star that accompanies the dawn.

>   Many have praised that timeless star,
>   which is not, however, the same thing as the praise
>   of an actually experienced star,
>   which must be by its very nature
>   essentially different from the other stars
>   if by no more than minuet of an arc.
>   Indeeed each is changed by it having been seen.

>   For those who are content to live in a timeless sea,
>   fantasy will quickly gloss the coming dawn with ease,
>   but those who are bound to the particular must humbly hope
>   imagination will come to unlock that mysterious bond
>   between the "it" and the "us."

APHORISM §19 A PURITAN POET?

———◆◆◆———

The Puritan would-be poet referred to in the preceding poem was Richard Dana (1787–1879), whose poem "Daybreak" occasioned it. Dana was the cofounder of the New American Review, which introduced American literary circles to European Romanticism and asked for an American response. This was well before Emerson had published "Nature," and Dana always insisted that Emerson's thinking was flawed by its "dichotomy between tradition and insight." Dana endeavored to find in the past "that spiritualizing power" that belonged to the heart and to the imagination. In attempting to square Romantic thought with traditional Christian orthodoxy, Dana anticipated the work of other American Christian Romanticists, including James Marsh and Caleb Sprague Henry.

Dana's attack on Emerson has been passed off as a matter of religious opinion. This is taken as a pass for moderns, since they consider religion to be a private matter that can be bracketed off from their or anyone else's thinking. But this is a serious mistake, if not for themselves, certainly for understanding the past and what is at stake in Dana and Emerson's disagreement. What is at stake is understanding the way that time holds together past, present, and future, which, as it turns out, is very much a germane question for us as well.

THE END OF THE STORY 1831

Ascending into the lofty isolation
>of the white wineglass pulpit of Old South,
>the youthful pastor, with a storied past,
>numbering no less than eight in his paternal linage
>who had graced the pulpits of New England,
>stanched himself and with a pregnant pause
>surveyed the faces of his expectant flock.

The story that confronts him that day is the one
>that begins, "On the night in which he was betrayed,"
>which is, even for him, an oft-told tale.
>It continues, "He took bread," and so on, ending
>with an invitation to come to communion.

He has come that particular morning to tell them
>that he can no longer participate in that story with them.
>Oh, he was not quibbling about doctrine, he assured them,
>which had been debated and parsed with no end of insight.
>No, what he had to say was that he could not allow himself
>to be defined by a story, this one or any other, for that matter.

He needed to be free, he argued, from the entanglement of story.
>He would not be defined by a story,
>not by a sacred story,
>not by a national or a family one,
>not even by the one of his own making.
>The point, he went on to say, was that one could not be
>an independent self and resort to stories
>that began, "I was born," "My parents were,"
>or "When I came of age, I ..."

He would tell them that he needed to be "a transparent eye"
>through which nature itself, unstoried,
>would determine him and him alone,
>on account of which he would be the self-reliant man.

At his descent, the congregation sat stunned,
    and the world took note.
    Exchanging the pulpit for the podium,
    the pastorate for a new identity,
    the American Scholar,
    the Sage of Concord,
    the definer of the American self,
    the quotable source of wisdom
    unbound by historical context,
    in spite of the fact that at Old South the story did not end;
    in spite of voices like those of Hawthorne and Melville,
        who struggled to restore and revise the story;
    in spite of a civil war that turned individuals into causes
        and young men into armies that marched to the beat of the
        drum.
For thirty years, he continued to be self-reliant
    and the arbitrator of American life,
    which was a testimony to his strength
    or maybe his somewhat sad irrelevance!

APHORISM §20 LIFE BETWEEN POLARITIES

American life has been lived largely between polarities, groupthink and individual-think, between democracy and aristocracy. The problem is that it is very difficult to know when one is an individual-think or has become part of a groupthink, likewise for knowing if one is an aristocrat or a democrat. Hence comes the fear of the slippery slope. One unguarded step, and you are the opposite of what you thought you were.

One way to reduce the hazard is to partition the world into separate spheres. For example, in politics one should be democratic, and in another, say academia, one should be aristocratic. This, however, simply transfers the question to the question to what is politic and what is academic, about which there is no little confusion.

Clarity will lie in finding a unity that transcends the polarities. The search could be mounted by taking an example of something that appears to be primarily aristocratic—that is, where the best rule and the goal would appear to be excellence. In the field of music, a practitioner is encouraged to excel, to be among the best. In that manner, a flutist might accomplish great virtuosity, but the result might prove to be unmusical! What is missing in the portrayal of a great flutist is that besides the reaching for excellence, she or he is imagining in his or her mind retrospectively the music that the composer intended and prospectively the music that the audience will experience. This concern can be understood as a quest for communion—communion with the past and future.

Communion arguably is the common ground between the polarities. It embraces the excellence of the individual and the needs of the others at the same time. It is the intangible quality of music, the emotion of the story. By means of communion, the polarities may be successfully navigated without the fear of the proverbial slippery slope. Where is communion to be found in American life?

INDEPENDENCE AT ONE HUNDRED 1876

Samuel Clemens climbed the stairs
> to the gabled tower of his new-build Victorian Gothic,
> imposed on the bucolic woods of the Hartford farm
> and on the prim colonial Beecher house next door.
> He secluded himself in that house's man room,
> equipped with billiards, a bar, a humidor, and a teletype,
> in order to become once again Mark Twain.

He needed in the most urgent way to write the great American novel,
> to free America from the thrall of European Romance,
> to earn recognition as an author ranked world class,
> and to restore health to his flagging finance,
> drained not a little by the maintenance of this very house
> and the sustenance of his standing in Hartford society, which was
> the arbitrator of America's flourishing publishing industry.

When his pen touched the paper that day, it found a river,
> the one that connects the North and the South,
> which divides the East from the West,
> and which was the seminal artery of his youth.
> Having traveled in thought a thousand miles,
> and retreated in time a span
> sufficient to revisit his youth
> and to be securely before
> the outbreak of the hostilities
> that became the Great American War,
> in which it slaughtered six hundred thousand of its own.
> His pen launched a raft on which he had set two characters,
> a homeless boy and a runaway slave
> bound by the common need to escape
> with the vaguest sense of to what:
> to freedom and a self,
> which seems at first to go by the name of Cairo.

There the raft was to be abandoned,
and they would go their separate ways.
As it happened, which is hard to explain, they missed the turn at Cairo
and the north-by-east way to their destinies.
I suppose it is not totally beyond imagination to accept
that a boy and slave might, in some preoccupation or confusion,
miss the impact of the Ohio River
on the larger muddier stream of the Mississippi,
but it is difficult to imagine how the author
on the bridge of the great gabled house
would not have seen the turn as they passed.
This left them to drift down the river
where every slave feared being sold,
down which the boy had no self to be found,
but which the author, given his storied muse,
could find an easier course to sound.
So as a result, the boy and the runaway slave continue to drift,
occasionally venturing along the way through
the tragedy and folly of American life,
through the "good" and the "bad" slaveholders,
the kings and dukes, the charlatans and rogues,
the violent and cowardly mobs,
only to return to drifting nowhere.
With no possible destination in sight,
no turn left by which one might go upstream,
and no way to imagine an ending in a sea beyond this America,
Samuel Clemens, it seems, realized that he had no choice
but to return to the story that he thought he had left behind,
his youthful *Adventures of Tom Sawyer.*
What Huck and Jim could not do for themselves,
Tom would have to do for them, not, of course,
without the comic flare enshrined in his mind,
the very European Romance that Clemens,
but evidently not Twain, had left behind.

The Sawyer solution would be no less than a tilting with windmills,
        planned and executed not as La Mancha's knight-errant,
        with the remnants of an ancient chivalry,
        but with the bravado of the European Romantics,
        Scott's Ivanhoe, Byron's Childe Harold, or Dumas's Cristo.
        In the end, Jim was freed, and Huck became himself
        not by means of Jim's escape, or Tom's machinations,
        but by the fact that Jim's owner, Ms. Watson,
        back upriver in Missouri had him made him free—
        nor by means of Huck's ingenuity or Tom's tutelage
        but by the fact that Huck himself wrote a book,
        out in the West, where tales hung like low fruit on the tree.
Are we, then, to understand that European Romance was to blame
        for the Great American War?
        Was it not true that in the end
        things had turned out
        the way they had to be?
        And the war a tragic romance
        best to be forgotten as somehow un-American?
        So it would seem that in the year 1876,
        the centennial of the American independence,
        everything was found to be well and good, just as it should.
Why, then, does it seem that
        somehow, someway, someone
        is selling us down the river?

APHORISM §21 A MISSED TURN

※━◆━※

Had Huck or Jim or Twain spotted the point where the clear water of the Ohio flows into the muddy waters of the Missouri, the two would have gone east together, and, God forbid, they might have ended up on Samuel Clemens's doorstep, so pleasantly located on the Hartford farm right next door to Harriet Beecher Stowe! The result would have been that America might have known something about itself in 1876, something that even now it fails to know.

APHORISM §22 RENAMING: MEMORY LOSS OR GAIN

※━◆━※

Americana has been shaken by a rash of topplings (e.g., Silent Sam, the statue of a Confederate soldier upended by students on the campus of the University of North Carolina in 2018) and renamings (e.g., Grace Hopper College, formerly Calhoun College, at Yale in 2016). Do these efforts represent an attack on memory launched by some political correctness? Any legitimacy to be lent to this claim must reckon with the fact that such namings and erections were the product of the twentieth century, Silent Sam being erected in 1913 and the college named Calhoun being created in 1930. It would seem that these were not so much the fruition of memory as a strategy for navigating social change in America.

That means that they are properly subject to question. What in fact had they intended to say? Is that still an acceptable part of our present conversation? The answer to that question cannot look away from the rise of virulent racism in the early decades of the twentieth century. The presumption is weighty that these were not the result of memories but messages freighted with racism: "Challenging white supremacy will not be tolerated." Less blatant, as in Yale's case, the message was "Yale wants qualified students from the South." These students would be, without a doubt, young white men from families of wealth.

To whatever extent memory may be lost by removing statues and renaming institutions, a larger memory stands to gain.

Dale Nichols, *I Cultivate My Garden*, 1940,
Krannert Art Museum, University of Illinois at Urbana-Champaign
(Image is available online.)

MAN IN HIS GARDEN: AN EKPHRASIS

The land is saturated with time,
      which explains why it seems to flow
      like a swelling sea or drifting snow.
      What else could account for its frozen energy,
      or the puzzling fact you could not go to the spot
      where the artist stood and framed the scene,
      for whatever place that might have been
      has long been planed and cleaned
      of its orchard, haystack, and trees,
      monochromed into a motionless sea
      in which any so precious an eighty has ceased to be.

At the time, eighty acres was all a man could want,
      indeed could even handle with the hand of a wife and a child.
      The eighty was the world to him,
      which, in the end, would bury him,
      as he quite well knew,
      but he loved it just the same with all his being.
The assent of the singular diminutive man
      is hardly noticed upon a first or casual look,
      being nothing more than a short black hook
      on the diagonal line running left to right,
      just below the bright red barn,
      the center of the artist's remembered world,
      followed by its lengthening shadow,
      stretching down, even as the man leans up into the light.
      Once seen, it is impossible for him not to be seen

and to know that in truth that it is he who is the theme
of the artist's dream.
Like a coiled spring, he presses upward,
hands a-splay, firmly gripping the paired oak handles
of the single high-wheeled Kentucky—or is it Missouri?—"mule,"
sending rhythmic thrusts of force to the rack of tines,
two on each side of the gap that straddles the green lines,
uprooting weeds and casting up waves of loose dirt,
to cup the roots of each of his carefully seeded rows,
and he is saying to himself as he goes,
    "I cultivate.
        I cultivate.
            I cultivate my garden."
Observer, as you pass by, do not think of this art
as a ploy to kindle some kind of nostalgic glow in your heart.
After all, it was 1940 when paint was laid to this canvas,
two years past the worst farm crisis this country has ever known,
heat wave, drought, dust bowl, market collapse,
and one year before the dark winds of world war
would unfreeze the nation's will,
bringing an end to its self-afflicted wound,
and in the midst of all of this,
this slight twig of black,
which first lived in the artist's soul,
is saying, "I cultivate.
        I cultivate.
            I cultivate my garden."
No, this artist has painted not nostalgia but faith, daring, and hoping,
as a call for some kind of resolve in your soul
    to cultivate,
        to cultivate,
            to cultivate your garden.

A COMPARATIVE EKPHRASIS ON TWO MOUNTAINS

Mountain 1
Marsden Hartley's *New Mexico Recollections #15*,
Joslyn Art Museum, Omaha, Nebraska
(Image is available online.)

Beneath a clotted sky, a serrated line of mountains runs.
    Washed in primal ocher, and streaked with Venetian red,
    sent by a rising—or is it a sinking?—sun.
    In the center of attention stands a single mountain
    swollen like a fountain about to burst.
    Above, the sky churns, making clouds tear.
    Behind, mountains flow, raising a rhythmic cheer.

If all this sound and movement seems to you to be too queer,
    that a mountain or a sky, being an inanimate thing, unlike us,
    would be so moved, the artist would remind you
    that, once, this desert floor was lifted and folded
    by some ancient hidden force now spent.
    It flowed like dough and rolled like a drum.
    And even now, if you had time to watch,
    your eye would see the mountains move about,
    and if your ear could reach below its threshold,
    it would hear the pulse of a guttural drone.
    Thank this artist for allowing you see what your time won't
    and for letting you hear what the acuity of your ear can't.

So it might seem that this art has no need of an ekphrasis!
    It is clear that skies and mountains are living as much as us,
    and the artist appears to recollect in this colored scene
    that he has neither need nor wish to be further seen.
    Says he, "Poet, please, keep silence with me."

As it turns out, art can be both happy and sad,
to which, if you will allow, I would like to add
by way of a personal note that when I die,
write not my name across a Ruscha-like sky
but take my ashes to a Hartley-like mountain.
There, deposit them in some fold, where
      the sun might touch them with Venetian red,
      the sky might wet them with a tear,
      the rock might hold them in its line of cheer.

Mountain 2
Word/Play, an Ed Ruscha Retrospect, Joslyn Art Museum, 2018
Lion in Oil
(Image is available online.)

The visual precision of the camera takes in the outside world
and prints it out in a negative form, which can be altered
in a series of clever steps, by time spent in the dark,
where light can be switched with shade,
color enhanced, lines crisped,
none of which nature can do itself,
given the canvas and time on which it must work.

As you move about this retrospect, does it not begin to dawn
that you are looking not at mountains but at the images of mountains?
If you are not yet convinced, look at the mountain behind the lion.
It is half a mountain completed by its mirror image.
OK, you knew that right away, but does that not make clear
that you are looking not at mountains
but at images that have come out of the box!
The mountain has been silenced, so you expect that it is text that talks.
But the epitaphs for CLARENCE and CLAIRE are not to make you weep,
and STANDARD does not announce a standard someone intends to keep.
LION IN OIL, being a palindrome, is not a clue to look for a lion or for oil.
The texts like the images are each a trompe l'oeil.
It might seem that this art has no ekphrasis to descry.
Not so—poets are seldom found without some reply.

So listen carefully. Between the silenced word
and the silenced mountain, a cry can be heard,
from a boy, I think: "Does anybody see me?"

PATERSON: A REVIEW OF THE MOVIE, 2016,
Directed by Jim Jarmusch

In *Paterson*, bus drivers write poems,
  housewives do art in their homes,
  and actors play in neighborhood bars.

On the way to the bus, the driver walks down
  caverns of redbrick walls erected
  by the manufacturing of another day.

The bus runs down streets lined with little shops
  once stocked with must-have merchandise
  but now reduced to the last-chance sort of things.

The run is broken by a lunch break next to a mostly hidden waterfall,
  which reminds one that the present clutter of *Paterson* was spread
  over the breadth of a breath-taking stretch of natural order.

The driver writes his poetry in a secret book
  and holds it close to his heart.

The housewife's art hangs in her house,
  curtains her shower and drapes her body.

The actors play in the neighborhood bar
  before the *Paterson* Wall of Fame.
  On the Wall of Fame hang a plethora of black-and-white pictures
  and yellowed news clippings of *Paterson*'s past greats,
  poets, artists, and performers who rose up out
  of its web of humanity to national acclaim.

It is clear that the bus driver's poems will never travel beyond his home,
  nor the women's art, apart from her cupcakes sold at the farmers' mart,
  nor will the actor's play ever ascend the boards of the great white way.

It is not that *Paterson*'s humanity has somehow declined or changed
  but that the America around it has reduced its need for poets, artists, and actors
  to a few megastar types, overcompensated and shamelessly idolized.

PESD
(Post Election Stress Disorder)
November 2016

———◆◆———

Love

I love my country deeply,
>   but I have no illusion of it being a paradise,
>   nor can I abide talk of its exceptionalism.
>   I am thankful for our president-elect for he makes
>   it possible to see just how homely and flawed it is.
>   For a lover,
>>   this simply makes one love it more, Poor Jack stuff.
>   As for others,
>>   I don't know—more tolerant, one might hope.

Served

We who have served—
>   we have apparently elected one who has not served but used.
>   Is that because we regret our service?
>   Or is it perhaps that we hope, at least, vicariously,
>   to be among those who use?

Lines

God can draw straight lines with crooked sticks.
>   We have given him a handful, haven't we?
>   Hopefully he will be amused to be so challenged
>   and we will be doubly amazed in the end.

Played by the Russian Bear?

I am thinking not about
those anemic liberal dupes of the past,
"com-simps," as we derided them,
but of red-blooded warriors of the present,
"neocons," "America Firsters," and the rest of that gang
who have danced, consciously or unconsciously,
to the tune played not, of course, by communists,
God forbid, but by the newly minted oligarchs,
whose playbook is taken from our own.
I guess that makes them "com-spires."

In the State of Illusion

Listen, my children,
     in the State of Illusion,
     there shall be universal access to health care.
     Our neighbors will secure our borders at their cost
     and buy our goods at our cost plus whatever.
     Our power will again be absolute,
     for the world has been told to take care of their own,
     and the media, that our alternative facts are better than theirs.

And should your ever fear your president
     is not all there or that he doesn't really care,
     just wait for the tweet in the night.

Babel

It is said the builders of Babel had one form of speech and few words,
     which was quite adept at building towers but not so much at writing poems.
     This appears to be the case with government by tweet, at least in regard to walls,
     Which gives rise to the thought that we seem bent on returning to Babel.

PESD REVISITED

July 4, 2020

—◆◆—

As painful and humiliating as it has been,
the Trump thing appears to have been necessary,
for America has been sitting on a pile of unresolved issues—
race, poverty, brutality, sexual exploitation—
that have now come to a head.
It is unclear what results will come from this,
but it is not going to be easy to put this back under wraps
until some substantial changes are made.

In the annals of the buffoonery of strong men,
it now seems that we Americans have produced a worthy peer,
and might well boast that our version has out buffooned them all,
which I must admit has been not a little worrisome,
save for the fact that at the same time he seems to have set
a record for the greatest degree of underachievement.

APHORISM §23 ON BEING GREAT

Curiously, the labeling of something as "great"—for example, Alexander—is a means of identifying the beginning of a decline and belongs to fantasy more than honest analysis. So much for wanting to be great again.

Was it not in the end a tragic distraction that took Greeks to the Indus River when their real future lay in the north and the west? Is it too much to suggest that the large swath of the east all the way from Alexander's lost tomb in the Libyan desert to the Indus River lacks local development because of, to no small extent, Greek imperialism? Remember how frantic the Jewish resistance was against Antiochus Epiphanes? Observe how Greece itself has languished on the south east margins of Europe. The case can be made that they were instrumental in bringing it upon themselves. Haven't we all paid a price for such greatness?

So one wonders whether we are not now distracted form that which is most central our destiny, and whether, if we indeed become "great again," it would be the beginning of our decline.

APHORISM §24 AT WAR

When you are at war with the world, you will soon discover that you are at war with yourself.

ULTRA-MARIS

Tancredi Overseas

———◆———

"Somewhere beyond the sea,"
along the northern shore
of that isle at the end of the Italian boot,
on a cape named for its famed paladin, Orlando,
      dubbed Furioso, who, upon recovering his sanity,
      tracked Aramante, the vilest of medieval villains,
      to the isle of Lampedusa, where he left him slain,
is the very place where the last prince of Lampedusa
had taken resort with his aged and ailing mother,
driven to do so by the Allied bombardment
that struck the Port of Palermo in April 1943.
In that attack, a wayward bomb struck the Palazzo,
on the Via Lampedusa, their ancestral, but dilapidated, home.

So on the Capo d'Orlando, they waited out the storm,
which would once again change everything,
as the Risorgimento had the century before.
The prince knew that their way of life was about to give way
to a new order about which they would have little if anything to say.
So he sought some sanity in his memories of bygone days,
working out a story in his head about the way that past transition
had been navigated, or could have been navigated, by the late last duke,
Don Fabrizio, with the slyness of a fox, which fitted his name,
who had distinguished himself from his peers on the right
who refused to give into the change
and were consequently dashed on the rocks,
and from his peers on the left
who chose to sell out to the change
and were washed out into the sea of oblivion.
Fabrizio's scheme centered on a youthful successor

who would swim in the Risorgimento by doing a little of both,
the handsome, charming, and cunning Tancredi,
who the last prince was attempting to flesh out
for his legacy novel, *The Leopard*.

In July of that year, the Allied landing came,
despite an ill wind and tide, on the low-lying beaches
of the southernmost shore between the villages of Gela and Licata.
The American's Seventh Army brought with it a Tancredi,
a real one, as youthful, charming, and handsome as the imaginary one,
wearing a corporal's stripes, and part of three-man team
that carried and fired an 81-millimeter mortar,
whose purpose it was to clear the way for the advance
of the tanks of the Second Armored.

This Tancredi was fresh from a small Vermont farm,
the youngest boy in the family of ten,
whose parents had come from Italy in 1901.
Italian was still the language in the home he was raised.
His preparation for war was, one might say,
high school football,
part-time jobs fixing cars at the filling station,
stocking shelves at the local general store,
the hard physical work of dairying from dawn to dusk,
and, of course, running the woods with his brothers on a hunt.

The mission of the Seventh was to drive across the low-lying center,
ninety miles of hilled terrain cut by streams
and woven together by ancient roads that spun
like overlapping spiderwebs,
in order to deny the port at Palermo to the enemy,
who were intrenched on the straits that separated the island
from the mainland, behind what they called the Etna Line.

Once the Seventh had secured Palermo,
they pivoted and raced down the coast

to the straits of Messina to own the island itself,
which meant that they would pass through the Capo d'Orlando,
where Lampedusa cowered dreaming of his Tancredi,
scarcely aware of the foreign presence.
In fact, the Seventh did on the seventh of August,
with the real Tancredi on point, focused on the job to be done,
scarcely registering the marks of alien land, except
perhaps for a fleeting smile when a mate named the place
they were passing the Cape of Orlando,
to whom he softly rejoined, "That's name of my oldest brother.

At the straits of Messina, Tancredi would recall
Patton driving past saluting them, "the lowly GIs,"
a moment they all relished, to think that one as high
as the hard-charging, pistol-wearing general had saluted them,
just before they were all packed up and redeployed to England.

On D plus one, this Tancredi and his buddies
stepped onto Omaha Beach and hunkered down
till the breakthrough came at Saint-Lô.
Then they were again on the run, laying down mortar fire
down the border of Belgium out into the outskirt of Aachen,
on the heels of the fierce and desperate defenders.
It was there that he was wounded and sent down
to the hospital unit, only to return to his unit,
at his insistence, and back to the run,
until, wounded again, he was sent home,
overwhelmed by the exhaustion that caught up
up with him once he stood down.

Back in the States, he found that his world was changed,
ever much as that of the prince whose path he had crossed
without either one being aware of the other.
The supply chain built during the war
meant that dairying in Vermont was on the way out,

as its textile industry, which would be bought by Goldfarb and sent south,
as its machine shops, which competed in an industry
dispersed across the nation,
as its rustic puritan ethic which was replaced by the sovereign consumer.
Yet the resourcefulness that had distinguished him as soldier
made him a formidable survivor in the Vermont of outsiders,
tourists, persons of means, seeking picturesque respite,
and creative individualists, seeking fulfillment in the purity of craft.
Many of his peers were at war with this change; he was not.
Many of his peers sold out to this change; he did not.
But in his quiet, persistent way, he navigated a path that zigged and zagged
like a mortar unit on the front, never letting go of deep things in the land
of his birth.
Paired with a Vermont girl with deep Vermont roots
who he met at a Woodstock dance, he fostered and coached a family of kids
and received from them a bounty of grandchildren
who all live and work in the heart of a new Vermont.

Like Lampedusa's imagined Tancredi,
he was able to bend and yet snap back.
The former lives on in a story
that Italy recognizes as one of its greatest narratives.
The latter lives in the reality of Vermont
and is the source of my story of an American soldier.

APHORISM §25 THE TRANSITION NARRATIVE

Among the literary masterpieces of the world, one of the key forms is the transition narrative—that is, a narration that takes place in the transition between one way of life and another. At the head of Western literature stands the novel Don Quixote *by Miguel de Cervantes, whose story line traces its way through the replacement of the age of chivalry by the age of Renaissance. At play in such transitions are those who try to hold on to the past and those who sell out to the future. Holding on to the past is, of course, always an illusion. Cervantes understood that the popularity of the accounts of the chivalry was a means of denial—a fantasy used to escape reality. What would happen, he pondered, if anyone were to actually attempt to live the life found in the accounts of chivalry? Comedy and tragedy were bound to follow. To most, the don was a joke. To the clerics and scholastics, a disease to be analyzed and cured. To the duke and duchess, something with which they could entertain themselves. Curiously, the future belongs to none of these. The clerics and scholastics will pass into irrelevance. The duke and duchess will be dashed on the rocks. The popular take is that the don is the hero because he dares to dream the impossible dream. But the don dies, not a little because of the rejection and abuse of the world. Out of the mix, it is Sancho Panza who actually, if grudgingly, learns something. Isn't he the person of the future, taking a measure of the don's nobility into the future? One could add to the list of works that qualify as transition novels. Suffice it to say, transition narratives are very much in need by the world of change in which we find ourselves.*

APHORISM §26 BEING WESTERN

The essence of being the Western world does not, of course, belong to the Western world. Therefore, it is quite possible for that essence to show up somewhere else—say, in China! There it will not necessarily look identical to how it was realized in the West, but it will be essentially the same thing.

APHORISM §27 REN, OR THE MAN CHOOSING

⋙◆⋘

The Chinese character Ren stands for the primary attainment of the followers of Confucius, and it is variously translated as "authoritative," "exemplar," and "consummate," each of which seems to read a Western point of view back into the original genius of the Chinese insight. If one looks carefully at the character, one will observe that it is made up of two simple characters. The first is the character for "man." The second is the character for the number 2. Suppose "ren" had been written with the character for "man" and the character for the number 1. Then the ideal man would be a fanatic. This way and only this way. Or suppose "ren" had been written with the character for "man" and the number 3. Then the ideal man would be a relativist. This way or that way or maybe yet another way. But it strikes me that a man who can see both sides and then choose is the ideal man, the true Confucian. I would translate the character Ren as "one choosing" or perhaps "the deliberate one."

APHORISM §28 THE DREAM AND THE RED CHAMBER

⋙◆⋘

Is it possible to dream your way out of the Red Chamber?

She began to hear Baoyu shout abusively in his dreams, "How can," he cried, "one ever believe what bonzes and Daoist priests say? What about a match between gold and jade? My impression is that it's to be a union between a shrub and a stone!" (Dream of the Red Chamber, *chap. 36, p. 705).*

Baoyu, the boy born with jade in his mouth, navigates the palace looking for the door to the outside, where an alternative destiny, one of his choosing, might lie. The end becomes unclear, but in reality, the search is the answer.

FRAGMENTS OF THE
SPIRITUAL NARRATIVE

APHORISM §29 MYTHIC OR MECHANISTIC

The mind seems bound to fly from mythic to mechanistic thought as if there were nothing in between, such as a ground for a different kind of thought that might make it possible for a narrative to take off or, better, to be joined.

APHORISM §30 THINKING HONESTLY ABOUT GOD

An a priori philosophy and a positive revelation are the Scylla and Charybdis of the attempt to think honestly about the self and God. The poet philosopher Friedrich Hölderlin made this point more than two hundred years ago, writing to a friend, "Properly speaking an a priori philosophy, entirely independent of experience, is just as much nonsense as a positive revelation where the revealer does the whole thing and he to whom the revelation is made is not even allowed to move in order to receive it, because otherwise he would have contributed something of his own" (from letter 61 to Sinclair, Homburg, December 24, 1798).

Modern is an orientation to the present, to things as they are now. Who, then, is not modern?

The best moderns are those who base themselves in a narrative about what is being left behind, as well as how they are moving on, by means of a reference to an imagined future, even if it is a somewhat vague utopia.

The worst moderns are the postmoderns, who disdain narrative.

Christianity's effort to cope with modernity has been by no means a stunning success, but arguably it has done better than any of the other historic religions. It is, after all, the mother of modernity, even if it has not always and everywhere been willing to recognize its child and it has consistently refused to name its father. This poor little bastard, even in his maturity, has been disowned by its own children the postmodernists, who like to think that they were born straight out of Minerva's head.

THE UNDONE NARRATIVE:
VIRGIL IS CALLED TO THE COURT

Comes the vaunted poet,
    renowned for his florid celebration
        of Italy's green countryside,
        of the plow, whose share opens its fertile dirt
        of the sower, whose cast feeds it with the precious seed
        of the reaper, whose scythe gathers in the harvest bountiful,
    summoned by the Augustan court to be its poet,
    for who better than him can one imagine
    for the inauguration of the dawning age?

Where, pray, will the fabled muse send him?
    Back to the verdant soil of the *bel paese*?
    To its watered hills and mountains lined with trees?
    To its celebrated rugged plowmen and its dauntless ingatherers?
    No, no; the muse, it seems, has sent him to a distant shore
    where once a storied city stood above the Dardanelles,
    until it had been leveled to the ground by the treachery of its foe
    and had cast a mythic remnant on a hostile sea in search of home.

Strange it is that a myth made a thousand years in the past
    should hold the hope of a new and lasting age.
    Yet the specter of the erased city haunted those times,
    and what glory could be imagined that is not that city?
    In it was found that which holds all meaning,
    and, without it, the undoing of everything.
    So the task seemed clear to the poet—
    he must from that very fate exempt this new Rome!

On Latium's volcanic coast, the poet set a sacred stage
    on which the land could be baptized.
    The Trojan War would be reenacted on this shore,
    a new Ilium, little more than military camp, built there
    that would defeat treachery and escape, if narrowly,
    the specter of the age, the disappearing city.
    Everywhere blood would be poured
    in heroic volumes on that land,
    a fit libation, a virtual baptism of blood.

What celebration greeted that finished poem,
    what laurel was lavished on the poet's brow,
    and how long the poet's shade has endured!
    Still did not his poem bend a dawning age back
    on an ancient dark and make the new old?

The new age would come only when someone
    could find a way for blood to become life.

THE MAKE-DO POET

We set sail from Troas.
—Acts 16:11

———◆———

This make-do poet lies on his bed
  and ponders pieces of poetry in his head,
  poetry about a journey that could bring light
  to that oft-told story that to many has grown old
  but to him is yet young and wanting to be retold.

  Could it be that he, too, is called to be God's poet?
  To use his broken verse,
  so unlike the heroic hexameter,
  to inaugurate an age yet in its dawning?

In the ancient times, he recalls, it was in the end
  not the storied Virgil but the obscure physician
  who best saw what was poised to change the world.
  Luke wrote it not in proud hexameter but in prosaic meter:
  "We set sail from Troas," he began, and, with that, I think,
  left Troy behind.

  With those words, he began his eyewitness account
  of an east-to-west crossing of that oft-traveled sea,
  all of which before had failed to make a beachhead
  for the east or set in motion a transformation for the west.

  Not returning Greeks loaded with plunder.
  Not defeated Trojans steeled with honor.
  Not imperial Persians backed up by their triremes,
    whose failed crossings, in the end,
    simply lured the west into the east.
Not the flower of Macedonia driven by the one called Great,
    and who lies buried in the sands
    that stretch from Issus to Memphis,
    left haunting a land with dreams of glory
    that fell like broadcast seed,
    accomplishing nothing but the occasional
    sprouting of some exotic weed.

When that anonymous "we" was announced as sailing from Troas,
    did he who wrote it have any idea
            of what was about to transpire?
            Of to whom that line would someday be sent,
            you, O Theophilus?
            Or of how many others, after you,
            down what length of time, would read it?

To the enlightened some of our day,
            these narratives deserve deconstruction,
            allegedly causing a bondage to a false past,
            and/or an incitement to a nonexistent future.

To this bent poet on his bed,
    these narratives churn kaleidoscopically,
    reconstructing falling fragments of imagination,
    giving him a hope that he might rework them once again.

If, O Theophilus, you are still out there, he would for you
    with a midwife's hands wipe away the blood of birth
    and wash the infant in waters crystal clear from the aboriginal sea
    and say to you again, "With this brief transit, it all began."

APHORISM §32 SACRED TEXT

Misreading the Bible comes down to the confusion between magical acts and theological acts.

DIFFERENT ACTS

A magical act is a manipulation of matter,
    a rabbit pulled from a hat,
        a saw passing bloodlessly through a glamorous gal,
            a Houdini escaping from a double-locked cell.

A theological act is alteration of a relationship—
    a sea is parted,
        bread is multiplied,
            a tomb is emptied.

APHORISM §33 UNREAD

More often than not, the text is unread by the pious, little more by the liberal reformers who find in it things to be changed, by conservative reformers who find in it things to be enshrined, or by mystics who find a depth behind it. Mostly the text is a beggar begging to be read.

WHEN DAVID

When David and his warriors
took that Jebusite town called Jerusalem,
it was hardly a great fortified city,
but it was fiercely defended.

The city sat on a modest mountain
on the east edge of the fertile Shephela.
It started at the top, anchored to a shrine,
and then ran down the ridgeline
that fell off to the south,
which allowed it to bask in the noonday sun.
It was well watered, graced by the ample flow
of a spring on its east ridge that rose above the valley.
A tower defended it from an attack from the east
and an attack from west block by a wall known as millo.

When David made the city the head of his kingdom,
he brought with him singers and dancers.
After all, it was well known that he was one too.
It is incredible to many that such a modest
unmonumented town could become the source
of a substantial literary accomplishment,
but perhaps that overlooks the power
of a king who sings to stir memory.

The fact of the text has been a stumbling block
on which many a wise man has tripped,
unwilling to imagine that a race might trust script
more than displays of power built out of rock,
which apparently is what happened in a realm
that began with a king who sings.

A LEVITE LAD

or

Imagining the Composition of Psalm 42

Far from his home, a Levite lad of Korah's clan
pastured his father's bulls in the valley of the balsam,
watering them from the hidden springs that dot that land,
during that dry season that comes before the early rains.

It was a sacred trust, the care of these unblemished beasts,
destined for sacrifice in Jerusalem at the coming feasts.
Here they would fatten on the abundance of the golden grass
when in the pastures at home the grass was withered and passed.

In the evening light, he would sit and read the swallows' flight,
marveling at the strange way they'd feed on the fly.
He would try to decipher the whispers of the evening breeze
that once had spoken to David from atop these very balsam trees.

Then he'd turned to mimic with his harp the rhythms and notes
of the falling dark: the coos of doves, the wild dogs' howls,
the snaps of burning logs, the flutter of the wings of preying owls,
and the anxious cries of thirsting deer in search of the water brooks.

When the lad at last lay down, some sleep to find,
the surfeit of things passing through his mind
were too much to let sleep come with its needed remedy,
and so he would seek some peace in the shelter of his memory.

"I remember," he would tell himself, "how, with the throng,
my voice had praised and thanked my God in holy song,"
and how he had passed with solemn step into God's house
while on either side the maidens of Israel had lithely danced.

Sleep would come somewhere in those pleasant recollections,
but not for long, and awake again, he'd ask as if in a dream,
"When shall I appear again before the face of the living God,
for whom my soul thirsts like deer thirsting for the living streams?"

The gone sleep, he told himself, must be repaired,
and so he would again return to his memory: "I shall remember,
wherever I am, be it on some unnamed mountain of the south
along the Jordan's flow or in the green of Hermon's timber.

"I shall remember how the dancing multitude fell still
when their leader had asked to pass through the gates of righteousness:
'Judge me in your mercy so I may be brought unto your altar.'
And they all had echoed back, 'Even unto the God of my joy and gladness.'"
At the dawn, he played on his high-pitched harp to wake the day,
and then he would turn to practice making letters in some wetted clay.
He wished he could make them say what he had thought that night
so that he might give them to the world to pray in its sacred rite.

WHEN I PRAY THE BOOK OF PSALMS

I

When I pray the book of Psalms,
       I keep company with the Hasidim.
       Together, we eat the bread of heaven,

      with the wisdom editor who framed the psalms
          and taught us the law from Aleph to Taw
          and bid us in hearts to recite them day and night;
      with the performer who sang above the lyre
          asking why the nations did conspire
          against God and God's Messiah;
      with the suffering servant on the rack of pain
          who called on God's name,
          crying out, "My God, my God";
      with the Levite who walks the field panting
          as does the hart for the water brooks
          and longing to walk again in God's house;
      with the shepherd king who himself did sing and play the harp
          to honor the God, who nimble made his feet
          and taught his hand the art of war;
      with the dethroned king asking God to remember
          the shortness of his life when considering
          to unhide himself and quench the fire of his anger;
      with the children beside the waters of the Babylon
          who on the willows hung their harps
          yet kept Jerusalem's song within their hearts.
Longing all for that deliverance when we the Hasidim
      will rejoice in glory and will sing joyfully on our bed!

II

Still in this, our day of waiting,
>we together pray the book of Psalms
>as in a wilderness we tread the pilgrim's way,
>and together drink the living water from the rock,

>with the accommodators, first Jesus, then Peter, Paul, and John,
>>Augustine on the Afric shore as Rome was coming down,
>>and Rashi, who in Christendom's Champagne vinted kosher wine;

>with the translators, first the seventy-two diaspora Jews, who rendered them in koine Greek,
>>then the solitary in a cave with a lion at his feet, who made them sing in vulgar verse,
>>and the friar on the river Cam, who made them march the cadence of English speech;

>with the chanters who sang the ambrosial rite in cathedral chapters,
>>the Benedictine brothers, in Gregorian mode,
>>the black-robed ones murmuring the Znamenny of the east,
>>the baroque choristers in the chord progressions of Purcell and Blow,
>>and the songsters in the gracious melodies of Gelineau;

>with the commentators, the senatorial Cassiodorus,
>>the great Gerhoh of the golden commentary,
>>and the brilliant rabbi ReDaK of medieval Jewry,

until our deliverance comes
>and we the Hasidim will rejoice in glory
>and sing joyfully on our bed!

THREE PROPHETS

I would tell you a story of three prophets
of that obscure race who lived between the great powers,
the people of the Nile to the south,
and people between the two rivers to the north.

First is Elijah the Tishbite, a rustic swept up
by a wandering band of prophets
and set down in the kingdom of the north
for the trial of fire.

Second is Isaiah of Jerusalem, a royal lodged
in a scribal school on the ground adjoining
the temple and court of the kingdom of the south
for the making of text.

Third is Jeremiah of Anathoth, a priest drawn
by the masters of the text into the struggle of the parties
of temple and court as the kingdom makes its last stand
for shedding of tears.

Who together sketched a line of prophetic speech
that turned this obscure in-between people
into the baseline of the world.

I

Elijah the Tishbite

Once, Israel's prophets hung out in bands
that supported a seer's way of life.
They wandered up and down the land,
free and not a little wild,

and sometimes taken with frenzy—
remember how the youthful Saul
had joined them in their dance.
It was in the time before the text,
when prophesy was not a word
so much as it was an act,
remembered in the oral lore
kept by the prophetic bands.
It was in such that one named Elijah had begun.
He chose a Yahwist band who had thrived
until the foreign queen sought to bring them down,
which made him a solo on the run.
He hid in the wadi of Cherith,
he hid with the widow of Zarephath,
and yet he ran the king down to issue a challenge.
After his victory on Carmel, he ran deep into the Negev,
where he lay down to die
yet rose at the encouragement of an angel
and ran again all the way to Mount Horeb,
where the still small voice sent him back
to anoint Hazel, Jehu, and Elisha,
which signified three coming deaths,
the last of which being his own.
In truth, his zeal and his heroics frighten the band,
who often ran from him as once with him,
and who could never again contain him.
Yet just when they would feel safe from him,
he would return to trouble them, and so it is no surprise
that in all its many manifestations,
Israel could not get past the idea that he would return.
So, in the end, when his work was done and his end had come,
the Yahwist band returned and followed him down
to where the Jordan flows beyond Jericho,
telling the young Elisha that his master would be taken,
and, upon Elisha's return, confirming his ordination,

after which they bequeathed their lore
to the historian of the north
whose sacred text the ages have read.
Hence, we ourselves can scarcely pass a year without
imagining that this Elijah is about to return and trouble us!

Isaiah: God Saves
Isaiah 7:3, 14:28

Isaiah had come to the school of Jerusalem's prophets
when he was still a boy, learning and laboring
in its scriptorium, mastering the skill of text making,
copying and building text that lay out on parchment pages.

The vision of that ancient school swept across a broad horizon.
It looked to south to the Cush, to the Isles of Tarshish in the west,
to waters of Babylon and the mountains of the Medes in the east,
            and to the highlands of the Hittites in the north, where Assyria was rising.
They saw that the old order in which Israel had begun was ending.
The local order in which it had been competing,
Ammon, Moab and Philistia, Damascus and the Northern Kingdom,
would soon be assumed into an imperial order
and Jerusalem's future would be arbitrated from afar.

They saw that this change was of God, even as they were of God,
and who they would be in this future would be of God as well.
In time, a word had come onto their pages,
shearim, meaning something like a tenth, or a remainder,
which allowed them to imagine a way through that change.

It was progressively clearer in the school that "the tenth" would come
by attrition—plague, famine, and war—
but in the end "the tenth" would restore
faith to Israel
and, more, teach God's ways to all the nations.

The boy, once he became a master of the word, married
a daughter of the prophets, herself being a master of the word,
and when a son was born to them,

they named him Shearim, Shearim yashuv!
Remainder, Remainder Restored!

Their problem was how what they saw could be taken to the world,
a problem that became worse when the old king died,
shaking the school's connections with the court of Jerusalem,
for the new young king displaced the elders, the wise, the skilled
and seasoned warriors and replaced them with his peers.

It was then that the young man spoke up and said, "Send me.
I will intercept the king when he visits the fountainhead,
and I will tell him not to fear the spent forces of the old order.
I will show him my son, Shearim yashuv, who is our future!"
and that even now that a maiden is conceiving a son,

The young king, Ahaz, chose that day not to see the future that stood before him,
the child named Shearim yashuv, and still less the child
about to be conceived, whose name would be Immanuel,
as the school warned him, "Seeing he will not see,
and hearing he will not understand."

So it was until the year Ahaz died. When that staff was broken, Isaiah cried,
"Let not Israel's enemies rejoice," for from the ancient root
a snake would come forth, and on the hill an ensign would be planted.
The staff of the new king, Hezekiah, would be raised up,
and he would bid the nations to come through the noble gate.

Not Knowing
Isaiah 6:9

Father, how could they not know?
You sent Isaiah to Judah so it could know its not knowing.
I came into the world so the world could know its not knowing.

Yet your world is not made up of unknowables,
any more than your covenant with Judah was made up of mysteries,
which is to say that their not knowing comes from choosing not to know.

Isaiah prophesied so Judah would know its not knowing was their choice.
I was crucified so that the world would know its not knowing was its choice,

for only in seeing one's not knowing is one able to break free
and know, really know.

Oh yes, Lord, now I know, I know.

Jeremiah: The Man beyond the Text

The young man had grown up in a small village called Anathoth,
        three miles north of Jerusalem, halfway, as it were,
        to Bethel and not so much farther to the ancient shrine
        Shiloh, his ancestral home, he being of priest lineage,
        albeit diminished for passing through
        Eli, the high priest, who died in a fall;
        Phineas, his son, killed in a battle;
        a mother, lost in childbirth;
        and a son, born without glory,
        under the cloud of the lost arc
        and of the demise of Shiloh itself,
        a Levite in the land of Benjamin,
        on the line where the kingdom
        had come apart, divided between a north and a south.

As a boy, he had gone often with his father
        to stand among the priests in Jerusalem's temple,
        his father being exceedingly proud of him,
        and he being secretly uncomfortable with the show,
        except when he managed to sneak out
        to where the congregation of prophets met,
        in the outer grounds of the temple's precinct.
        There he felt comfortable with himself,
        mostly absorbing the words and the cadence
        of prophetic speech, until the day came
        when he could not *not* speak, and then uttered.
        that first "oracle of Yahweh," raising brows,
        exposing his drceit to his father,
        and earning the enmity of the priests of Anathoth.

What he said that day caught the ear of the noble family
        of Shaphan, who would successfully navigate the treacherous sea
        of Israel's life from King Josiah's reforms to that day when his grandson,

Gedaliah, was made governor of the remnant remaining in the land,
Jeremiah included, after Jerusalem had been destroyed by Babylon.
They had heard in the young prophet's voice the language and tone
of the recently discovered book that had launched the reform.
     Which explains why the priests of Anathoth had so quickly
          condemned their own, since the reform had deprived them
               of their high places and put them under Jerusalem's thumb,
and who had noted in his assertion of a boiling pot in the north,
a credible threat of which they should keep track,
     which explains why they recruited from the family of Mahseiah
          the young scribe Baruch to record the prophet's words
          in a book, in case they might later prove true.
This gave Jeremiah the clout to catch the notice of the temple priests,
     which explains why Pashhur, the temple's secretary, banned this outsider
          from the temple court, since the priests insisted that things were under control
          and that no change need come to what they had done from time immemorial.

The partnership of Jeremiah and Baruch responded to the ban
     by making a book, a list of oracles and laments,
     which the prophet had preached and prayed, to be sent
     to the very congregation before whom they had been said one by one,
     but now amassed and much closer to being fulfilled, Babylon now at the door,
          which explains why when it was read in the hearing of the people,
               the leaders were alarmed and asked that it be read in the presence of the king,
who ordered each page to be burned as it was read in his presence, apparently thinking
               that by doing so the word would be undone,
     causing the prophet to re-dictate the word to the scribe Baruch,
          making it clear that the word could not be undone,
          and that he was the servant, the suffering one,
          would show the way for a life in God
          to be lived beyond the text!

Indeed, that scroll of 605 became a core around which
     a number of subsequent layers of text were wound,
     a biography of the prophet by the scribe Baruch,
     a historical commentary by the historical school,
     and then countless dabblings by many other hands
     as late as the Greeks, earning the scroll the reputation
     of being overly large and largely in disarray!

To what purpose, one wonders, unless somehow
it was to keep Jeremiah in the text, which, as we have seen,
he was already beyond, so that the bottom line of scroll
is not the famous Jeremiads so frequently used by the life haters
but the life lived beyond the text that continues to give comfort to life lovers.

APHORISM §34 THE PEOPLE OF THE BOOK

The orientation of Israel to the text, which led to the sobriquet "the people of the book," is usually dated to the postexilic community, and, more specifically, to Ezra's reading the Torah at the Water Gate. This has fed the cause of the minimalists who argue that authorship of the Bible belongs to the Persian period. But this overlooks the important text event, which is preexilic, dating to the year 622 BCE. During the reign of King Josiah, the high priest Hilkiah produced a book that he claimed to have discovered in the course of renovating the temple. This text is generally understood to be all or part of the book of Deuteronomy as we know it. On this text Josiah based a sweeping reform of Israel's religious and political life. Seventeen years later, his son King Jehoiakim was also presented with a book. This time it was a book of the prophesies of Jeremiah, recorded by the scribe Baruch. The king dramatically consigned its pages to the fire burning in his winter quarters, cutting off successive portions of the scroll as they were read to him. Apparently, the king believed that the words deprived of a text would have no power. With this event, it is arguable that the text has arrived as the arbitrator of Israel's life.

At the Table of History

Judah was run over by no less than five empires,
not to mention the latter-day colonialists and national socialists.
They are all gone, but Judah still sits at the table of history!
Tell me that this does not have something to do with text.

APHORISM §35 BEYOND THE WRITTEN TEXT

———◆———

Behind the written text is flesh searching for meaning. Beyond the written text is flesh living its meaning. It would appear that the written text, if not absolutely essential, is substantially instrumental in flesh living its meaning. Once when I was at a ballet performance, it struck me that the Odette was not a beautiful woman in a seductive pose—art had transformed her into a communication, a meaning, a word. This seemed to me to be a clue to the incarnation; the word becomes flesh in order that flesh might become word. I have avoided a capital at the beginning of word for fear that lends itself to a mythological view, which fails to grasp what is at stake.

MARY'S JOURNEY TO BETHLEHEM
A Meditative Narrative for the Seven Days Preceding the Nativity

———◆———

Introduction

There is nothing like a story about a journey to capture one's imagination. Journeys promise some kind of self-discovery, and they populate our dreams. At the same time, they are often the metaphor of choice for trying to describe the nature of the spiritual life.

Spiritual writers of all traditions have made use of the theme. There are a number of Christian classics that have used Moses's journey to Mount Sinai as a model for meditation. Other journeys so favored have been those of Elijah to Horeb, Mary and Joseph into Egypt, and Jesus and the disciples to Jerusalem. This latter story was a motif developed by Luke for his Gospel, and it is a common theme for Lenten sermons and meditations.

There lies in the Advent season an implied journey that would seem to offer an equally fruitful metaphor for the nourishment of our souls. I am referring, of course, to the hasty journey of Joseph and the pregnant Mary from Nazareth to Bethlehem in the fading days of the year.

To those given to hard facts, this journey will seem too ephemeral to merit such a serious consideration. That this journey took place in December relates to the absence of any direct knowledge of when Jesus was born and the presence of some knowledge about the political factors some three hundred years later that favored setting December 25 as the date of the birth. That this journey took place because of a census or tax enrollment in Palestine ordered by Augustus is not supported by any secular evidence found to date. That this journey took place at all rests on accepting Luke's explanation that in addition to well attested fact that Jesus was raised in Nazareth, Mary and Joseph lived in Nazareth prior to Jesus's birth. This varies from Matthew, who explained the family's presence in Nazareth as the reaction of Joseph to the news that Herod the Great's son Archelaus had succeeded his father as the ruler of Judea and, as such, posed a threat to them.

On the other hand, not long ago, the media reported that construction workers laying a pipeline through the controversial Har Homa housing project just outside Jerusalem had unearthed a large rock around which an octagonal church had been built in the fourth century. The accidental find has been identified as the Kathisma, the seat venerated by ancient pilgrims as the place where Mary, heavy with child, is said to have rested on her way from Jerusalem to Bethlehem. The rock is, of course, a hard fact. But like the supposed birthday of Jesus, Mary's resting on the rock is a fact *for us* only insofar as we are willing to accept the testimony of Christians living three hundred years after the birth of Jesus.

The point of the story, I am proposing to tell, is not a pretense to knowledge about things but a hope for imagination in the midst of things. It is the hope that a metaphor can help us overcome the various forms of immobility that threaten our souls in their waiting.

When weariness besets our souls and we are ready to read it as a sign that we have chosen wrongly, imagining our souls to be on a journey can help us reinterpret that weariness as a traveler's weariness, an honest tired, which comes with the incline in the road, and which is always most intense just before one reaches the crest of the hill.

When pain stabs our souls and we want to back off from our thoughts because they have become too painful to bear, imagining our souls on a road enables us to recognize that this pain is nothing more than the rock that strikes against the foot. The soul can own the pain as a signal that it is alive and on the way.

When a hard place in the bed won't permit the sleep that restores and heals, the soul can imagine itself to be on a journey where that hardness is the stone that has been given to it for a pillow.

I invite you, then, to accompany Mary, the maid of Nazareth, on her journey to Bethlehem. This journey assumes that Joseph and Mary traveled for seven days a little over twelve to fifteen miles a day. Each day of the journey is marked by Mary's meditations, which are built on one of the seven names of the Messiah. These are the names that are celebrated in the seven antiphons that were written as introductions to the chanting of the "Song of Mary" in the daily prayer of the church during the week preceding Christmas. These antiphons, written in the seventh century, before people were so intent to claim authorship, were later gathered together to make up the well-known Advent carol "O Come, O Come, Emmanuel."

Day 1
Wisdom from on High
From Nazareth to Shunem

Mary slipped out of Nazareth with the apprehensive blessing of her aged parents, Anna and Joachim. Following Joseph's lead, she had taken the back door out of Nazareth, the steep narrow ravines that work their way down and out onto the great plains of Megiddo. The steepness of this path had forced the pregnant Mary to walk on foot, raising the question in her mind whether she would be able to cope with this journey. But just when her doubts seemed greatest, she found herself on level ground standing next to her husband. According to Joseph, there would be only a few places ahead that would require such a difficult descent or ascent.

Venturing onto this plain was like venturing onto the sea. The towns, whose names she had heard mentioned—Nain, Chesulloth, Megiddo, Taanach, and Jezreel—like Nazareth, sit on its edge, up in the hills, on either side like tiny seaports. Part of the reason for this was the ancient habit of not building on the flat and fertile ground, and part of it, perhaps the larger part, was the instinct for safety. Over centuries, armies had washed down these plains in regular intervals, leaving behind dead kings, Josiah, Ahaziah, Sisera, and Saul, to name but a few.

Stepping out on this great flatness stirred in Mary's memory the story of the ancient Canaanite army led by Sisera. It was a story she had listened to many times as a child. Her recollection of the story, reenforced by the sudden exposure of the plain, brought on a fresh wave of anxiety. Was this all that wise—that she, that they, were trying to be in Bethlehem before the end of the year, given her condition and all?

Literally, they were crossing the ancient battlefield. Though she had never been here before, she knew from the stories to look to her left, northeast, to the ascending ground, down which an ancient ancestor, Barak, had led his makeshift army of Israelites. The chariots of Sisera had bogged down in the wetland on which her feet were now seeking a firm footing. Farther in the background stood a conical mountain, off by itself, appearing to be an island separated from its coast. There on this mountain, called Tabor, the prophetess Deborah had gone and stood as the Lord had commanded her. She had summoned Barak and had sent him into battle. Behind Mount Tabor would be the oak where Heber the Kenite had camped. Sisera, leaving behind his broken chariots, had sought safety with the Kenite, not reckoning with the fact that this Kenite had a Hebrew wife. Jael had welcome him and lulled him to sleep, and when the defeated and exhausted Sisera slept, she drove a tent stake through his skull.

Mary's lips sang softly the song the women of her village had taught her:

> Most blessed of women be Jael,
> the wife of Heber the Kenite,
> of tent-dwelling women most blessed.
> He asked for water, and she gave him milk.
> She brought him curds in a lordly bowl.
>
> She put her hand to the tent peg
> and her right hand to the mallet.
> She struck Sisera a blow.
> She crushed his head.
> She shattered and pierced his temple.
>
> He sank, he fell, he lay still at her feet,
> where he sank—there he fell, dead.
>
> So perish all your enemies, O Lord!
> But may your friends be like the sun
> as it rises in its might. (Judges 5:24–31)

The words caused her heart to smile for the first time that morning. Reminiscences about learning these words as a girl made her cheeks warm. Clearly some things were being implied to her about her womanhood and its capability about which no one had ever spoken openly.

For the first time since she had entered the broad plain, she looked ahead, to the south, where they were going. There was Mount Moreh. To the north of it stood the village of Naim, and just to the south, Shunem, where they intended to stay the night. Would they find a shelter there as gracious as the one given to the prophet Elisha by the widow?

The distance to that goal—five miles, she guessed—renewed her anxiety. Were they wise to be risking so much, and for what? A line in a census book that would read "Jesus, son of Joseph, son of Heli, the Bethlehemite, of the house of David and the branch of Jesse." Her mind curled around the word *wise*. What kind of wisdom lay behind the imperial government's demand that a census enroll everyone? Numbers of people would choose to remain nameless by ignoring the state's order. Numbers of people would be further riled by having to do so. In the end, would the numbers and lists of names make the government any better or fairer or more acceptable to the people? Not likely. It was because of this "higher" wisdom of the state that they "had" to be enrolled. This having to be enrolled meant that she, now nearly nine months pregnant, was alternately walking and riding a donkey some eighty miles to a place she had never been.

Of course, it wasn't just the wisdom of the state that was to blame for this. There was also the wisdom of men—that of her husband, Joseph, who had determined the path and the timing. All summer, Joseph had gone back and forth on the question. He talked about ignoring the census. It would be a fit act of rebellion or at least a fit form of passive resistance to the Romans not to do so. Yet becoming part of the anonymous people of the land was most distasteful to Joseph. He could have enrolled in Nazareth as a displaced Jew. If he did so, his name would be further dissociated from Bethlehem and his Davidic heritage. What would that matter, for the child he was accepting as his firstborn was not his anyway?

Mary replayed in her mind the many times Joseph had gone through the argument with her only to confirm inaction. She reviewed these conversations and her part in them in order to discover what had finally produced Joseph's decision to have the child enrolled in Bethlehem so that he could be called a son of David. Perhaps he had simply worn himself out. Her pregnancy and the rapidly approaching end to the year of enrollment left one final chance. It seemed to her, from what little experience she had of such things, that it was the wisdom of men to procrastinate till only one option remained. Then they seemed to seize on this last chance as if it were proof of whatever wisdom was necessary to justify doing it.

Mary smiled self-consciously, careful not to let Joseph see. Her thoughts slid suddenly to the wisdom of women and her own role in what they were doing. She replayed the scenes of herself patiently listening to her husband go on, letting him talk, implying with her silence that she had no strong opinion of her own. It was her wisdom to let it take as long as necessary for her husband to make his decision and then to support it, whatever it turned out to be. She saw that she had carried out perfectly the wisdom that her mother had taught her, but somehow that very wisdom had not kept her from the precarious position in which she now found herself.

Here she was on this very lonely road in the middle of this great plain, burdened with a pregnancy that still puzzled her, trying not to let her discomfort show, and wondering if she was not somehow injuring her child or herself by the effort it took to go on. The conflicting wisdom of the state, of men, and of women swirled in her head with little hope that some sense might settle out of the storm.

Without opening her eyes, she felt Joseph's presence closer than it had been in the room they had occupied in her parents' house. She sensed a pride in his step that had been missing the last nine months. In that same darkness, she felt Deborah singing, Jael smiling, Barak crying, and a host of her ancestors shouting. Coming toward her she felt the heavy tread of the wandering prophet Elisha. For a thousand years, they had risked all in this valley of decision. Suddenly, Mary felt not exposed but surrounded.

A wisdom descended. It was not hers. Nor was it his, Joseph's. It was certainly not the wisdom of the imperial state. Nor was it the wisdom of her ancient ancestors who had fought and sacrificed in this valley and who were as puzzled as she was about the purpose of life. This wisdom seemed not to replace as much as to highlight pieces of all these lower forms of wisdom and then transcend them. It held out to her a purpose for this effort higher than any of the ones discoverable in the purpose given in the lower forms of wisdom. In the wisdom of God, what failed to make sense from any of the other points of view made sense because she was with those who she was meant to be with. She was happy, and she prayed, *O, come, thou wisdom from on high, who orderest all things mightily; to us the path of knowledge show and teach us in her ways to go.*

When she opened her eyes, the gates of Shunem were before her, and she knew that she would soon be curled up in the warmth of an inn at the end of a first day.

Day 2
The Lord of Might
From Shunem to Rehov

The inn at Shunem was small but welcoming, and it was so close to Nazareth that they were still known. They huddled together in a corner of the room that turned into a cave, and there they ate a light repast. It was wonderfully warm, and the tiredness of Mary's body drank it in with great gulps. The widow who kept the inn treated them like family and fussed over her advanced pregnancy. Had Elisha himself had such wonderful hospitality here? All evening, Joseph anxiously rehearsed his plans with Mary. They would take off first thing in the morning and would bypass the large city of Beth-Shan, which the Gentiles called Scythopolis. Mary could detect in his voice his disdain for the Gentile city, the same as his attitude toward working in Sepphoris, to the northwest of Nazareth. As soon as they had skirted the walls of Beth-Shan, Joseph had said, they would head to the tiny village of Rehov. It sat at the juncture of two great valleys, the valley of Jezreel, though which they would spend the next day traveling, and the valley of the Jordan, which would be their way south.

Tomorrow, he had warned, would be a longer day than their first day. It would be a full fourteen miles, as he remembered it. But it would not have anything like the steep descent they had made upon leaving Nazareth, nor would the way be as lonely as it had been out on the plain. There would be plenty of other travelers on the road, which would help them feel less exposed. Mary, he had said, could count on riding on the donkey most of the day. She had said to Joseph in return that the day's journey had seemed to have toughened her body and that she knew she would be ready to go on in the morning. In a like manner, he had continued to muse about their journey as they waited for sleep to come to their overly tired bodies.

As sleep came, Mary had felt reassured and quite confident about the next day. Indeed, it started well. The first three miles were quickly accomplished, as Joseph had suggested, with Mary on the back of the donkey. But nothing had prepared Mary for the sight that was about to transfix her. It came without warning when they passed over a ridge where the valley fell away sharply to the east. She slid off the donkey to take in the most spectacular panoramic view she had ever experienced. In the early-morning sun, the Jordan River was like a thread of silver, broken here and there but continuing as far as the eye could see. The hills that nestled the river and hid it from time to time were green gold and themselves ran though wider borders of rich red golds. This vast golden valley itself rested in a wrap of purple gauze.

It was, she thought, like looking into paradise! Standing very still, a stillness that passed into Joseph and the donkey as well, she drank in her vision. Minutes passed with no movement. A shadow passed over them, cast by an east-traveling cloud. Suddenly Mary was aware that it was this very view that had lured marauding armies on as they had come to attack her people. It was their preferred route, and it must have whetted their appetite for destruction. The shadow had brought a chill with it. But the chill seemed more the result of an ancient Philistine army than of the weather. She turned to her right to look squarely at the slope of Mount Gilboa. She knew from hearing the story repeated throughout her childhood that it was there that Saul and his son Jonathan had mustered the army of Israel. It was Saul's plan to halt the army of Philistines at this crucial juncture and, therefore, keep them from sweeping down this choice highway on the people of Israel. All the might of Israel had been mustered on Mount Gilboa, minus, of course, David. She shut her eyes tightly, as if doing so would keep her from seeing the rest of the story; from seeing how the Philistines had crushed the army of Israel on that day; from seeing how they had slaughtered Jonathan along with the fallen army; from seeing how they had left the anointed king of Israel, Saul, dying painfully from an arrow that had pierced his side—how there on that mountain slope, Saul, the anointed one, had fallen on his own sword to keep himself from being taken alive. A suicide! "Your glory, O Israel, lies slain upon your high places! How have the mighty fallen?" (1 Samuel 1:19).

She mouthed the word of the ancient song written by David and felt in her womb the sharp protest of a new David. She opened her eyes and looked at the barren slopes of Gilboa. With a shudder, she hurled the ancient curse back across the valley. "You mountains of Gilboa, let there be no dew or rain upon you, nor bounteous fields! For there the shield of the mighty was defiled" (1 Samuel 1:21). The curse had apparently been fulfilled since these mountains of Gilboa appeared quite bleak in comparison to the golden valley ahead of her.

A thought nagged her mind. Why had the Lord of Might let the might of Israel fail that day? And, after that, to fail before the Assyrians, the Babylonians, the Greeks, and the Romans? Why?

The threesome—man, woman, and donkey—became unfrozen. Mary felt like walking. Joseph had placed onto the back of the donkey the bundle he had been carrying on his back, and they had resumed their progress. They were walking at a surprisingly rapid pace down the great decline into the Jordan valley.

The thoughts did not stop bouncing around in Mary's head. *If, Lord, you are the Lord of Might, you would not have let Saul and Jonathan fail on the slopes of Gilboa. If, Lord, you had come then, you could have stopped the might of the Philistines and of all those subsequent hostile armies. If … then today your people would have been saved from the weight of all this tragic grief.*

If you, O Lord of Might, came now … then Joseph and I would not have been pushed into this awful journey. We would be at home in Nazareth. My parents and my cousins would be showering me with attention as my day of deliverance approached.

The thoughts danced macabre in her head, so much so that she had not been paying attention to Joseph or anything around her. Suddenly she was aware of another shadow. It was the wall of Beth-Shan, where the Philistines had taken the body of Saul and hung it to taunt and shame the Israelites into submission. The vision of Saul's dangling dead body was like a branding iron, and its effect was a flow of energy into Mary's legs. This city would be soon behind them, and it would be only another three miles to their stopping place.

She started again to think, *If you would come now, Lord of Might,* and then she stopped. It seemed that there was something working her swollen legs. That something, she suddenly realized, had been there all this past day, and it was not her. What should she call it, if not "might"? And whose might was it if it was not hers? Was it his might? Had the Lord in fact come! And was this his way of answering the enemies of Israel—the march of a pregnant woman on swollen legs that would bring an empire to the ground and its armies to their knees? A lump closed her throat, and a moisture stung her eyes, and she prayed fiercely, *O, come, O, come, thou Lord of Might, who to thy tribes on Sinai's height in ancient times didst give the law, in cloud and majesty and awe.*

She continued to pray in this way that night, till sleep came to her in the tiny inn of Rehov, under the brow of Gilboa, at the entrance to valley of the Jordan, where they spent their second night.

Day 3
The Branch of Jesse's Tree
From Rehov to Zaphon

They had slipped out of Rehov at the earliest light. The sun all morning long had filled them with great comfort. It was only when the sun was directly overhead that they began to feel overly warm. The road took them across a wadi where one could see that former rains had sent water rushing with such great force that it had tossed boulders about on its way down to the Jordan. A verse of one of the psalms played in her head: "Depth cries out to depth, for the voice of your cataract, for your rushing water and tumbling rocks" (Psalm 42:8). They were lucky that the autumnal rains had abated. Joseph paused and directed Mary's attention to the wadi. He pointed to a spot eastward where the wadi fell off steeply for its final run into the Jordan River. "This," he had said, "is the wadi Cherith, where the prophet Elijah was fed by the crows." It seemed a little too convenient to be true, but Mary was prepared to believe him. She had seen a solitary crow perched high on a jagged rock nervously watching them as they had approached. The crow was, it turned out, the lookout for a colony of crows that she could now see below scouring the dry bed of the wadi.

Joseph had invited her somewhat ceremoniously to step off the road for a rest. There they could have a bite to eat. This invitation had surprised her because up to then they had scarcely stopped to eat at midday. She smiled an interior smile at the idea that he was expecting the crows to come and feed them, though, of course, they were on the run every bit as much as Elijah had been.

He had led her into the shade of a rock that jutted out of the bank and had seated her on a flat stone that seemed to make a natural bench.

Then Joseph had reached into his breast and produced a cake. It was made of almonds, dried apple, and honey. Such a delicacy! Joseph said he had chanced upon a woman in Rehov who had made such cakes and had bargained her down to a price he could afford. The extravagance overwhelmed Mary. It so refreshed her that she was nothing but thankful. Joseph had coyly told her that honey had put the shine back into her eyes. The luxurious cake was complemented by a cup of fresh spring water that Joseph had found flowing out of the ground a little farther up the wadi. The cup of cold water extended their rest so that it seemed almost lazy of them to have lingered so long.

The result of this unusually long pause in the journey was that they were overtaken by a passing family. It was a husband and wife with two older sons, a younger daughter, and a beast of burden. They seemed to stop and look around as if they would continue on. Then after disappearing briefly in the shadow of the rocks, they had suddenly plunged down the wadi, leaving their ass up on the road under the watchful eye of the young daughter. The mystery of what they were up to held Joseph and Mary's attention and made them forget their haste. In time, the senior members of the party reappeared with bundles of precious willow branches. Carefully these bundles were tied to the back of their ass, and each member of the family assumed a lesser bundle of appropriate size to bear on his or her back. There was even a small bundle for their little daughter. Off they went back in the direction in which they had come, filled with joy.

The location was apparently their secret, and they had left assuming that it still was. Joseph and Mary had remained in the shadow until they had left, so as not to trouble them with the thought that someone else now knew their secret. When they were back on the road, Mary looked down the wadi to where the family had disappeared. There she could see the stump of a great willow tree and the shattered remains of trunks that lay about it like broken bones. It appeared like a valley of dry bones. And yet she had seen the family take a supply of wood from that very spot. Enough, one might suppose, that it would see them through the winter months, keeping their cooking hearth burning and occasionally heating the single room in which they would all huddle on the coldest of nights. She had seen with her very own eyes the family take life from the valley of dry bones. That old stump had been the source of the family's fortune in sticks. And she thought, *The stump of Jesse.* Then she turned and said to Joseph, "A shoot shall come out form the stump of Jesse, and a branch shall grow out his roots" (Isaiah 11:1).

Joseph's face lit up at the words, and Mary was pleased that she had had the courage to say it out loud to him. She knew that he was obsessed with the idea that the child that she was carrying in her womb was just such a branch, or that he could at least be brother to such a branch. It was the conviction that had compelled him to undertake this risky journey. This journey was costing her a great deal of physical distress, and she knew that it was also costing her husband a great deal of mental distress to return to the home he had left for reasons that were never clear to her but that were obviously of great weight to him.

As they resumed the pace of the journey, a step faster perhaps than earlier, to make up for the rest they had taken, Mary repeated in her mind, *O, come, thou branch of Jesse's tree, free them from Satan's tyranny, that trust thy mighty power to save and give them victory o'er the grave.*

Later in the day, the valley began to narrow. The mountains of Samaria reached toward the river, leaving the passage on the west side of the river very narrow. That narrowness heightened the risk to travelers on the west side of the river. Joseph had explained to her that they would ford the river and travel down the broad east bank, on the road that was known as the King's Highway. It would be safer for them. They would stay that night at the village of Zaphon, which was accustomed to lodging travelers like themselves.

Soon they were passing through the ford called Abel-meholah. Here Gideon pursued the fleeing Midianites and slaughtered them when he overtook them. Here Elisha had chased after the fleeing Elijah hoping to receive Elijah's mantle as Elijah left on his heavenward flight.

As the day wore on, Mary's legs had begun to feel like stumps. Joseph had noticed and insisted that she ride on the donkey. "The donkey will have no problem bearing your weight," he had said to her. It was not the donkey that worried her. It was her husband. When she rode on the donkey, it meant that Joseph had to carry the great bundle that consisted of their sleeping gear and their few possessions. Yielding to his insistence, she let herself be lifted on the back of the donkey. In a long pause during which

Joseph prepared to hoist the burden on his back, she looked across the valley to avoid seeing his effort. In the late light of the afternoon, the landscape seemed to be studded with fallen trees and stumps. They appeared quite dead in the late fall, before the onslaught of the winter rains. The vision raised again in her mind the question of whether a stump could really come back to life. There were around her so many of the dead. Dead Midianites, dead kings, Sisera and Jabin, Oreb and Zeeb, and all their commanders, like Zebah and Zalmunna, dead prophets, dead villagers, dead trees. She thought somewhat bitterly to herself, *The problem with my people is that they remember too much. We live too much with the past. Can this past give the present anything new and living?*

The question that had once been put to the prophet "Son of Man, can these bones live?" bounced around in her head. Deep into this downward spiral of thought, she felt a sharp kick in her stomach. Life had spoken, and the words floated through her mind: *"O, come, thou branch of Jesse's tree, free them from Satan's tyranny, that trust thy mighty power to save and give them victory o'er the grave."*

Day 4
The Key of David
From Zaphon to Adam

The road south on the east bank of the Jordan was full of traffic, much more so than on the roads up to now. It was not as busy, of course, as it would have been on the occasion of the great pilgrim festivals, as Joseph informed her. Still there was a constant movement of people on the road with and around them. The travelers were also more cosmopolitan than they had been on the west bank. This multitude of other travels made her feel safe. They had been passed by a squad of Herodian soldiers moving, as Joseph had explained, from Beth-Shan to the Alexandrium. The Alexandrium was one of Herod's desert fortresses, like Masada, or the Herodium, which sat just outside Bethlehem. The Alexandrium sat in the Jordan valley midway between the Sea of Galilee and Jericho in order to control its commerce. Toward the end of the next day, they would see the cone, a virtual mountain, that Herod had built with forced labor.

To her, the Herodian soldiers seemed to carry the air of authority that one ought to respect. Her instinctive deference to the authority of the soldiers had shown in her questions about them, and it had caused Joseph to hide rather poorly his own feelings by answering her in a clipped, matter-of-fact way. Sometime after the soldiers had passed them, they spotted a group who looked like merchants traveling north toward them. As they drew near, it was clear that some of them were wounded. Joseph rushed ahead to meet them and quickly began to help them dress their wounds. The words between them and Joseph were cryptic, but Mary could tell that Joseph was understanding what they were saying with perfect clarity. A few words had told him what had happened. Mary slipped off the donkey and joined Joseph in helping the wounded. Slowly their story was sinking into her consciousness. The group had been stopped by the same Herodian soldiers who had passed them. Their answers to the soldiers' questions had not been satisfactory, so the soldiers had beaten some of them. The beatings were supposed to elicit the answers that the soldiers wanted, and they had gone on for a considerable length of time since the merchants had no answers to give that would satisfy the soldiers.

Why were the soldiers so insistent, and what had they wanted to know? It seemed that during the past week somewhere along this road between Beth-Shan and the Alexandrium, a similar squad of Herodian soldiers had been ambushed by a group of Zealots. One of the soldiers had been killed and several wounded. The way the group's spokesperson had pursed his lips as he recounted the story made it clear that the injuries to the soldiers gave him a great deal of satisfaction. It was clear to Mary that these merchants held these Herodian soldiers in great contempt. It was also clear that this news neither surprised her husband nor found from him any form of rebuttal. She had, of course, overheard her husband arguing with the men of Nazareth to the effect that Herod could not be the true king of the Jews since he was an Idumaean. Even if he were a convert to Judaism, he could not be its king because he was not of the house of David. She had thought that Joseph argued this out of fun or for pride in his own lineage.

Now she changed her mind. Joseph seemed to possess a seriousness about the matter that she had up to now underestimated.

After about an hour, the merchants resumed their journey north, and they south. Mary could not get out of her head the conundrum that those who were in authority did not respect the people and in turn they were not respected by the people, her husband included. How could one be safe in such a world where true authority was missing? How could one feel good about bringing a child into this world?

A phrase entered Mary's mind that she remembered overhearing Joseph use in his arguments with the men in Nazareth. He would speak of the "key of David." It seemed to name a hope, name a messiah whom God would send. This messiah would bring an authority that would respect the people because it understood that it was the task of a king to serve the people. In turn, this authority would be respected by the people because they would know that their lives needed to be under authority. Obviously, no man held this key of David—not the Herodians who would beat witnesses, not the Romans whose arbitrary reign was sending her on this arduous trip, not the priests of her own people who were more concerned about their share of the sacrifice than the prayers, and not the self-appointed Pharisees who judged everyone to be beneath them. With the sudden loss of her innocence, she found herself with no legitimate authority unto whom she could entrust herself. Was there nothing to do except wait?

She struggled with the puzzle. If this authority that was to come belonged to God, it would have already been here. How else could men have come to form an expectation about it, if it hadn't been with them once in some form or another? If it had been the eternal God who was that once, then he had also to be right now as well. Suddenly she sensed the authority that had no soldiers to enforce it, no priest to parse it, and no scribe to declare it corban. At the same time, she trusted her unborn child to the protection of that authority. Whatever soldiers did or failed to do, that authority would justify bringing her child into this world.

With her hands lifting her heavy abdomen, she began to pray. *O, come, thou key of David, come and open wide our heavenly home; make safe the way that leads on high, and close the path of misery.*

Joseph called her out of her thought. He wanted her to see that the palisades across on the west of the river were beginning to move away from the river and reopening a wide plain on the west side of the river. Soon, he told her, they would be able to recross the Jordan and resume their journey on the west side of the river. He told her that they would cross the Jordan River near the wadi Shu'eib some ten miles south of Adam, where once the river Jordan had ceased to flow. There, their ancestor Joshua, after whom they would name their son, had led the people who had wandered for forty years in the wilderness across the Jordan into the Promised Land with unmoistened feet!

She wondered whether the river would be so accommodating to them. At the very moment, Joseph and the donkey were getting their feet wet, for they were fording a smaller stream that flowed into the Jordan. It was known as the Jabbok, and it was here that Jacob had spent the night wrestling with an angel. In her queasiness from the starts and stops of the donkey on whose back she was riding as it explored the bottom of the river for a footing, she redoubled her prayer: *O, come, thou key of David, come and open wide our heavenly home; make safe the way that leads on high, and close the path of misery.*

Day 5
The Dayspring from on High
From Adam to Jericho

As the sun set, the Alexandrium had in fact come into view just as Joseph had promised. It was a mountain, and yet it was not a mountain. It was a perfect cone that stood out in front of a natural line of mountains on the plain that had been carved by the river. There was no mistaking that it was an artificial construction whose chief intention was to intimidate Herod's enemies. At the top of the truncated cone stood a circular fortress. In the fading light, the cone cast a menacing shadow across the valley.

Soon after sighting the cone, which had continued to hold their eyes, the weary couple stopped for the night in a tiny village. The village sat at the point where two rivers met, the Jordan, which they had been following since the third day of their journey, and the Jabbok, which flowed out of the hill country to the east. Mary mused that this village bore the name of our first ancestor, Adam. According to the scriptures, this ancestor had been formed from *adamah*, the reddish dust of the earth. Red dust in fact coated everything in this forlorn little village. In truth, the village itself was more dirt than village. There were in it only a few modest houses with no accommodations. The travelers were gathered in a grove of trees that stood just beyond the little cluster of buildings. Joseph had unrolled their belonging and used the great wool wrapping to form a shelter for them. He had tucked her in and joined the men around a fire for a while. She could hear their voices but could not make out any of their words. She could tell, however, from the rise and fall of their voices, the rhythm of words, and the sudden alternation between pauses and torrents that the men were talking politics. The conversation had gone on for some time before Joseph had returned. After he tucked a leather pouch of heated stones into the bedding at her feet, he had drawn himself close to her so as to combine their warmth against the growing chill of the night. In spite of the warmth, sleep was slow in coming to Mary.

And when it had at last come to her, it was troubled. She was caught in some kind of inner struggle that she could not name. In part, she attributed it to the effect of the menacing shadow of Alexandrium, which had disturbed her from the very first moment that she had caught sight of it. But also, she thought that it was from the way this place had caused her to remember the story about the angel who had interrupted her ancestor Jacob's sleep not far from where they were lying. It was there on the very banks of the Jabbok that Jacob had wrestled with the angel. Somehow the angel had slipped into her sleep as well and was forcing her to wrestle him.

All her life, she had heard the story of how her ancestor Jacob had wrestled with an angel. Whenever she thought about the story, it sent a tremor through her. If the precise message of the story had eluded her, it had always been clear to her that the message was very important. Somehow, she understood that right now that very message was being sent to her as well. Jacob, she remembered in one of interludes between sleep and waking, had been on a journey filled with anxiety much like her own journey. He was returning to his homeland and didn't know whether he would be accepted or even be safe. She was carrying her unborn child to Joseph's homeland and didn't know whether he or she would be accepted or safe!

Somewhere in the night, before slipping back into her sleep, which the angel was filling with struggle, she recalled her husband remarking, before they had lain down, "We are halfway there now." She remembered thinking to herself at the time, *When we get up in the morning and take our first steps onto the road, we will pass the point of no return.* She realized that she had kept the thought tucked away in the back of her mind that maybe, just maybe, Joseph would say, "This is a mistake. Let's go back home"—that is, her home.

Was the angel of the night trying to stop her from taking that next step? Or was it just the opposite? Was the angel there to keep her from thinking about any possibility of abandoning the trip and returning to the comfort of her home in Nazareth? How could she know? She slipped again into a restless sleep. After some time—maybe minutes, but then again, maybe hours—she thought she heard a voice say, "Enough of this. Let me go for the day is breaking."

"I can't!" she had heard herself cry out in return. "I can't. I can't let go!"

"Yes, yes, you can," the other voice said. "Yes, you can, for your name is no longer Mary of Nazareth, but your name is now Blessed."

As she let go, a sharp kick in her womb woke her. Immediately she knew that neither the wrestling nor the sleeping would return.

So she lay sleepless in that dusty dot on the edge of the wilderness. That which had troubled her sleep made her wakefulness doubly unwelcome. She propped herself up to take the weight off her spine. In doing so, she created a tiny window in the bedding. Through it she watched the distant horizon. Whether by chance or by some internal compass within her that orients humankind to the dawn, she had ended up lying so that she looked east. She watched the black slowly separate into two layers. The black below ended with an undulating line over which a mixture of reds and oranges had begun to flow. A dome of inky blue formed over the center of the line and seemed to be weighed down by the black above.

Her eyes opened and closed on waves of drowsiness. It seemed that they had opened precisely at the moment when the upper curve of the sun broke the line and sent a wave of light in all directions. Despite herself, a thrill shot through her. *The dayspring!* The word sang through her head: *O, come, thou Dayspring from on high, and cheer us by thy drawing nigh; disperse the gloomy clouds of night, and death's dark shadow put to flight.*

So there it was, a new day. Its light had thrilled her even though it belonged to the day whose coming she had dreaded. To the new that she had feared, her heart consented. Now the issue was finding the same consent in her body. It was not yet ready to move. A residual drowsiness took her away for a time.

When she woke from this gift of at last peaceful sleep, she realized that Joseph was already stirring about in the first light of the dawn. He was making ready for the trip. She rose painfully from the propped-up position she had assumed earlier as relief from the pain that had been taking hold of her back. When she had started to walk, she realized that she was limping. She had quickly attempted to keep Joseph from noticing, but she could see from a flash of anxiety in his eyes that he had noticed. She quickly had said, "I slept on my hip wrong. It'll straighten itself out shortly. I just need to walk on it a bit more." But he had insisted that she ride.

Out on the broad alluvial plain, they set course for the distant mound on which the great Canaanite city of Jericho had once sat blocking the entrance of her ancestors into the land. She felt a great burden lift from her. She had said to her husband, with her hands embracing her distended belly, "We are over halfway home," referring to Bethlehem, which was indeed her husband's home and the intended home of her yet-to-be-born son, but hers only by adoption. The needle of pain in her hip was still there, but it was, she thought, a happy pain.

Soon they were crossing the Jordan back into the land of promise precisely where Joshua had led their ancestors on the way to victory at Jericho. The warmth of the sheltered valley comforted her, and the sight of palm trees amazed her. The road passed alongside the great mound of earth on which the city of Jericho had once sat. It rose seventy feet into the air and even without its walls above. She felt intimidated by its massive size. On the other side of the road was a spring that must have been the main water supply for that ancient city. It ran out of the bank in a great stream of cold crystal-clear water. A group of women had gathered there to fill their water jugs. Drawing water with other women was a special sisterhood that Mary had always enjoyed. She had not been part of it since they had left Nazareth.

She slipped off the donkey without saying a word, undid the waterskin, and left Joseph standing in the road. Joseph realized she was headed for a place where he didn't belong. He stood with the donkey pretending to check its bridle and hooves. Mary joined the women and delighted in their admiration of her very pregnant state. In turn, she filled the waterskin, exchanged pleasantries, and carried the water back to the donkey. Joseph could see how much the moment meant to her and noted to himself that at that moment she looked surer of her womanliness than ever before.

As she returned to Joseph, a piece of broken glass lying in the dust caught the sun and flashed a beam of light to her eye. The memory of the day's past dawn came to mind, and she sung inside herself, *O, come, thou Dayspring from on high, and cheer us by thy drawing nigh; disperse the gloomy clouds of night, and death's dark shadow put to flight.*

Day 6
The Desire of Nations
From Jericho to Bethany

When Mary and Joseph arose on the sixth day, the intersections of the byways were already filled with traffic. Jericho was like that year-round. There were travelers, pilgrims, soldiers, and camel caravans coming and going. They came from and went back to all the nations of the world: Petra, Ethiopia, Libya, Egypt, Damascus, and Tyre. In her sleeplessness the night before, she had realized that the movement never ceased, not even in the dead of night. She asked herself, what was it that moved all these people to be so far away from home?

The easy sheltered walk down the Jordan valley was over. It was time for them to face the ascent westward into the hill country where Jerusalem sat, scarcely twenty miles away. The rapid climb was softened by the fact that Romans had built a road up the canyon known as the Qelt. Not only was the Qelt wide and paved, but it also snaked across the streambed that lay in the bottom of the canyon over bridges they had built. This moderated the climb, which nevertheless remained constant. It was for that reason Joseph had insisted that they stop at the end of the day some three miles short of Jerusalem, in the village of Bethany. His plan would save the final climb over the Mount of Olives for the next day. There was also the distinct possibility that they could stay with the kinsfolk of Mary who lived in Bethany. After all, her parents had made them promise to look them up. Their hospitality could assist them greatly on the final leg of their journey.

For most of the day, walls of rocks rose steeply on each side. From the wall various rock shapes stood out like sentinels. Beneath them, in the bottom of the canyon, sometimes to their right and sometimes to their left, and sometimes directly under them, streams of dark water could be seen rushing wildly to join the Jordan below. The heavy rains of December had begun and had brought a chill to the higher altitudes. It had been to avoid these chilling rains that they had traveled down the arid and sheltered valley of the Jordan River, instead of down the spine of the hill country, as they certainly would have had their journey been in summer. Joseph's strategy had paid off. The temperature had stayed moderate, and up to now, no rain had interfered with their travel. The flow of water below them brought the fear that the last day or two of their journey would be spent in rain.

All day, strange parties passed them, as well as met them. Mary had spent the day, especially when she was astride the donkey, studying people's faces. She played a guessing game with herself: Where were they from? Where were they going? What was it that moved them? What was at the heart of their desires? For certainly it is desires that move humans on such distant quests.

At times, their presence seemed like an invading army carrying them along. It was up this same canyon that so many foreign armies, from the Assyrians to the Romans, had come to despoil and seize Jerusalem. Why had all these people left their homes, and what kind of desires had compelled them, these nations, these kings and generals, these common soldiers and wanderers, to come so far to seek whatever they were seeking?

Near the end of the day, the road flattened out, relatively speaking, and they could see a ridge far off. Joseph explained to Mary that it was the ridge of the Mount of Olives. When they reached that ridge, they would be able to see Jerusalem spread out on the opposing ridge, a truly awesome sight, he had promised her. Mercifully, closer to them was a small village tucked into a pocket this side of the ridge. It was little Bethany.

The sight of the day's goal caused Mary to turn back and look at the road on which they had labored the whole day. She stood rooted to the ground. Her immobility was confirmed by a sudden addition of weight to her body. She had never felt so heavy in her whole life. Even her hands had taken on a new weight, so much that they seemed to be too heavy to stay connected to her arms hanging at her sides.

Joseph sensed her need for a pause. He resolved to let it be as long as she wanted. So he stepped out of her way and said nothing. She seemed to be studying the road over which they had ascended in the course of the day, as if she had to figure something out about it before she turned to the challenge of the last mile of the day.

The traffic reminded her not so much of an invading army, as they had seemed to her earlier that day, but of some kind of mystical procession of all the nations bearing gifts to Jerusalem and then on their return bringing from her the fulfillment of their desires. Standing astride the road, she felt herself to be one of the waiting towers of the city. Through her, the people of the procession would pass into Jerusalem, bringing their desires to her, to the city beyond her, which promised to be the proper end of their desires. In the back of her mind, she was hearing the cry of prophet Haggai: "I will shake all the nations, so that the desire of all nations shall come, and I will fill this house with splendor, says the LORD of hosts" (Haggai 2:7).

Could the "desire of all nations" find a home in Jerusalem, and if it did, in what sense would that desire fill the temple with splendor?

All day, the question had been eating at her: What was it that all these people wanted? Now it struck her as she watched their ascent that their desire must not be much different from her desire.

What was it that she really desired? Right now, she answered herself, she desired to sit down and not get up. She desired to be alone with her husband. She desired to have her child's birth behind her and to be at home in Nazareth. She could vividly picture herself resting in her room in Nazareth. She held on to and savored the vision.

She was honest enough with herself in forming this picture to see that when she was there having what she had just called her desire, she was desiring something more. It had always been that way. She had seen it with others as well. They said they wanted something, but getting it simply made them want something more or else. The nations appeared to know what they wanted. They wanted resources, grain, wine, oil, taxes, tribute, glory, and empire, but they were never satisfied. What was all this restlessness of humankind? Did anyone really know what they wanted?

The problem, she suddenly thought, was that human beings fail to recognize what it is that they really desire. That is why they keep trying to solve the problem by desiring first this and then that, oftentimes, inevitably, seeking it at the expense of others.

If one should ever find what they really desired, then they would be at peace. They would be at rest, still. They would not be seeking it at the expense of others. They could end this restlessness and at last rest.

And then she was still. Desire had stilled her. Her thoughts no longer traveled back to Nazareth or even ahead to Jerusalem or Bethlehem, to her husband or the end of her pregnancy. She had suddenly desired one thing, and that was God. It was God that was the desire of all desires. And God was there for her and at no one else's expense! The moment was filled with glory and splendor.

When the moment had passed, she knew she had to move, so she moved her right leg, and it carried her around till she was facing the hill where little Bethany was content to be nestled, in the pocket of a ridge, content itself to stay forever without a view of Jerusalem. Mary would have to wait until tomorrow to see Jerusalem, and tonight, hopefully, she could rest with some family. To still any further desires, or, better, to put them in their proper place, she prayed.

O, come, Desire of Nations, bind in one the hearts of all mankind; bid thou our sad divisions cease and be thyself our King of Peace.

Day 7
Emmanuel
From Bethany to Bethlehem

The stay in Bethany was profoundly refreshing. A brief inquiry on the edge of the village had sent children running, and in no time at all they were being led to the house in the village where Mary's young cousins Mary and Martha lived with their older brother Lazarus. After a hastily arranged supper, the winter evening had been filled with talk, much of it on Joseph's favorite subject—who was related to whom, and how far their genealogies reached back into Israel's past. As usual, it slid into the explanation of his own connections to the house of David. Joseph had exhibited a buoyance in the conversation that signaled to Mary that her husband's spirits were greatly revived. One could say that he was positively ebullient, considering his usual reserved manner.

She knew that it was because the goal that he had set for them was almost accomplished. If the baby had been born that night, and there were times when Mary had been convinced that it would, the baby would have been born in Judea, a short distance from royal David's city. That in itself would counteract suspicions about the child's heritage. Joseph, as a traveling Jew, had lived with such suspicions all his life. It would, of course, be even more assuring if the baby would be born in David's birth city and would be enrolled there on official tax forms. That would make their son's heritage in the house of David so secure that no one would ever dare challenge it.

Her cousins had pressed them to stay yet another day. They could spend, they had suggested, the Sabbath together. But Joseph had been insistent. They were only eight miles away from Bethlehem, and except for the last climb to the crest of Mount of Olives, it was downhill from there on! They would see Jerusalem wake up in the dawn, and they would be in Bethlehem well before the Sabbath arrived. Easily, Joseph assured them all.

In the freshness of the morning air, it all seemed certain that they would be in Joseph's city by late afternoon, just as Joseph had said. If Joseph's extended family would be as easy to find as Mary's had been in Bethany, everything would go quite nicely. They should be secure and warm and capable of waiting until the baby was born no matter how long it might delay its entry into the world. The anticipation of what she would see this day took Mary's mind off the weight of her body, and it seemed to her that she had floated up the ridge that morning. She was enamored with the idea of seeing for the first time the holy city of Jerusalem, and even more the great temple mound.

After an hour or so, she stood with Joseph on the crest of the Mount of Olives and looked at Jerusalem in the early-morning sunlight. The fact that the western sky was lined with black clouds, coming up the western slope from the sea, did nothing except to make the sun's effect on the city more dramatic. From that perspective, in that light, no praise of Jerusalem seemed too high. It was the golden city! She looked particularly long at the perfect proportions of the temple, high on the mammoth platform that Herod had built for it. The extravagance of that much flatness in a world where flat was almost nonexistent inspired awe. The Holy of Holies was on the farther side of the square. Closer toward her were the porticos that divided the court surrounding the Holy of Holies from the woman's court. It was there that she longed to be with all her heart. It seemed to her that if she could be there, she would be with God like at no other time in her life. It would be the experience of a lifetime. The fact that she would be in the woman's court looking through the portico and that she would be using her husband's or her male cousin's privileges to touch the Holy of Holies did not spoil the thought. She had been used to doing things that way for a long time. If she was with God, she could ask all the questions that bothered her right now. But Joseph had been impatient about lingering too long to look. Perhaps it was because he had been here before, or perhaps it was because his eye kept going beyond the city to the dark wall of clouds behind it in the west.

Descending the hairpin curves of the road onto the floor of the Kidron valley allowed successive glimpses of the temple square, each different, and each fired her imagination and longing in a different way. That longing was in direct conflict with Joseph's insistence that they had neither the time nor the money to go into the city itself. That would be even truer for a visit to the temple. All along he had rehearsed with her the plan that the thing to do would be to pass around the north end of the city, where they would find on the far side the road to Bethlehem. After her delivery, at the time of her purification, she could stand, like the native women of Judea, in the temple and personally offer the sacrifice for her purification!

She yielded to his reason, but her heart could not help muttering to itself, *I need to be with God now, before my delivery. I need to have my questions answered now.* She wanted to say to Joseph, "You really can't understand how I feel." But she didn't.

Rounding the northwest corner of the city wall brought another degree of chill on the couple. The black wall of clouds seemed to form a line across the hill road to Galilee that they might have traveled down, a hint of what they would have been up against if they had. The black cloud bank also formed a line parallel to the road that they would take to Bethlehem. Rounding the corner of the city wall not only exposed them to the west wind but also confronted them with the citadel and its three towers. Herod had named these magnificent towers after his wife Mariamne and his two friends Phasael and Hippicus. As they approached the three towers, they could scarcely take their eyes from them. It was only as they approached the Jaffa Gate itself that a disturbing ugliness drew their eyes away from the towers. It was a bare hill left in the corner of the wall just before the gate where the wall ran east. All the rest of the land outside the city was green and planted with olive trees, vines, or gardens. Pools of water were scattered here and there, ready for irrigating the landscape. The greenness even in winter made Mary think about paradise. What was this bare hill? Joseph explained in a clipped manner, which Mary recognized as a sign that the subject was disagreeable to him, that it was kept that way by the Romans who call it Calvary, the place of the skull. This was the place where the Romans executed those they considered criminals.

Mary pulled the great robe in which she was wrapped tighter to offset the increased chill, which came partly from the black wall of clouds to west of them and partly from the ugliness of the hill.

The road turned abruptly southwest, and they found themselves walking away from the city and the bare hill that the Romans called Calvary. The last miles were slipping away. At the three-mile post, the road began a southward slope, and one could make out from there the tiny town of Bethlehem. Alongside the road, there was an outcropping of rock that looked like a chair. Its back was toward the north, and its seat faced south, catching the full bounty of the noonday sun. Mary slid from the donkey and was drawn instinctively to this spot in the sun, which did not sway like the donkey beneath her. The warmth in the rock and the warmth coming at her from the sun, with its low winter zenith, began to work the chill out of her. The solidity of the rock caused the nausea in her stomach to abate. A pleasant torpor came over her. The only disturbance that remained was an occasional feeling of disappointment that they had not stopped in the temple. She had not had her chance to be with God. This now had to wait till later. Even if it would be only a couple of months, as Joseph had suggested, the delay felt the same as being asked to wait forever. The thought repeated itself: *If only we were with you, God, then we would understand, and everything would be all right.* Somehow her sentence got turned around in her mind, and she heard somewhere in her soul, *I am with you. I am* ... she had heard it in the sacred language of her Hebrew ancestors: *I am* immanu. God, the great *el*, had said it to her, that he would be with her, *immanuel*. Indeed, God was with them right now. However different their circumstance could have been, had they been in the temple, or had the child been born, or had the world itself come to an end, it would still have been the same *immanuel* that she felt in her heart right now. She didn't need to go back, or on. She could just sit here forever.

The fading of the warmth, now mostly drawn from the rock by her body and from the slackening rays of the sun, which had begun its decline into the last of hours of light on a winter's day, roused in her the thought that she needed to go on—for the sake of her husband, for the sake of the baby, for the sake of everyone else in the world who might be looking to her for something she did not recognize or understand. She rose and mounted the donkey and felt a different kind of pain. Would her child indeed be Sabbath's child? "Bonny and blithe, good and gay," as they say.

Joseph took the lead, to hide his anxiety from her. She studied the broadness of her husband's back and pictured being greeted by the members of Joseph's extended family, whom they would discover, or would be discovered by, after however long it might take. However, it happened, she knew that everything was the way it was meant to be and that the great labor of their life was about to be accomplished with the help of God. She mouthed the word: "O, come, O, come, Emmanuel, and ransom captive Israel, that mourns in lonely exile here until the Son of God appear."

THE JOURNEY OF JOSEPH AND THE FAMILY INTO EGYPT
A Meditation for the Days Following Christmas

⊰─◆─⊱

Contents

Preface

I readily admit that an attempt to tell the New Testament's story of the holy family from the perspective of Joseph is the product of my imagination. It is not near as fanciful as the visions of the late fourth-century patriarch of Alexander, Theophilus, who imagined the family's journey into Egypt as a string of miracles performed by the infant Jesus.

Very little is said about Joseph in the New Testament, and what is, is disputed by scholars. Beside outright invention, this account has been over the centuries guilty of a great deal of conflation. The Gospel of Luke located Jesus's stay in Bethlehem in a stable, and the Gospel of Matthew locates it in a house. Critics see this as a contradiction and conclude that at best either one or the other is true. My story accepts both to be true, creating a chronology that allows first the one and then the other. My purpose is not to argue a maximalist's approach to the Bible but to tell the story in a way that reassociates the reader with the story as it is told in the Bible.

In a novel by James Wood, *The Book against God*, Timothy Biffen, a fictional young theologian, defends his spare belief against the attack of the novel's protagonist with the confession that he does not have a clear either-or certainty founded on inner knowledge and that he had never had a vision or even heard God's still small voice in his breast. This concession is rather typical of moderns of most persuasions. We hear a claim in the Bible that God granted visions, auditions, or visitations of angels unlike anything that we experience, expect perhaps among the rarest echelons of the religious. Joseph, we are told, had an angel appear to him in a dream after the wise men of the east had left him. The angel is said to have told him, "Get up, take the child and his mother, and flee to Egypt and remain there until I tell you." (Matthew 2:14). Clearly Timothy is thinking of such a text when he avers to having no religious experience. But his conclusion has more to do with how the Bible is read than what the Bible intends to say.

There was a time when those who read the biblical text thought that such a claim identified what was perfectly common in their experience. Their association with the text was very different from the way readers in our age are associated with the text. Somewhere along the line of development, there was a conscious effort to disassociate the reader from the text. The text in that way became an object that confronted the reader. Those who were bent on commending the faith used this disassociation to produce submission. Since you don't experience such miracles today, it is necessary for you to depend on those who did. Those who were bent on disputing faith were equally happy with this treatment of the text. They could argue that since these events were so unlike anything that we experience, they are, if not false, irrelevant to our own lives.

My telling of the story of what happened to Jesus during his infancy and early childhood is simply intended to allow my readers to understand the events as an experience not too different from their own. My hope is that it might cause a reader to say, "I believe that Joseph was led by the voice of God, because I recognize that kind of voice in my own interior life." Indeed, that they might even believe that they could be or had been called to go into "Egypt," and to understand the Joseph story as somehow an everyman's story.

A Second Beginning in Bethlehem

When Joseph and Mary arrived at the gate of the town, the winter sun was well into its descent. The old men of the town sat in the gate, as was the common practice of the times, exchanging their opinions about the issues of the day. After Joseph had greeted them, he asked politely whether he might drink from the well that was at the gate.

"Ah," the most senior looking of the elders replied. "You know our town."

"Yes indeed," he replied. "I have longed to drink from the water of that well as once my ancestor David longed to drink of it when he was hiding in the cave of Adullam."

One of the other elders said, "Yes, those were bad times for our village. The Philistine garrison controlled our city. Blessed be David, who rose up and freed us from the hand of the Philistines."

"And tell me," Joseph replied after having slowly drained the cup of the sweet water, "is the garrison of the Herodian's still making this town free today?"

As soon as he had said it, he knew that he shouldn't have done so, for he could see the elders stiffen. He had to break the silence that his remark had caused.

"Once I lived here, and now I have returned with my wife. I am trying to locate my family. I am the son of Jacob, of the clan of Jesse."

The elders remained quiet and admitted only to the vaguest recollections of a Jacob, and certainly to no knowledge of how his surviving family might be contacted. Fortunately for Joseph there was also a group of boys hanging out at the gate, ready to run errands for the old men. For a small tip and a promise of more if they were successful, they tore off through the streets of the village in search of anyone who might remember Joseph. Not finding anyone who admitted to remembering Joseph, the boys grew frustrated and disappeared. Only one, the one who was not so well dressed as the others, returned to the gate where Joseph and his young, very pregnant wife waited.

The boy was apologetic for his failure and had not wanted Joseph to wait any longer. He tried to give the money back to him, but Joseph thanked him and even gave him the extra coin he had promised.

In the presence of the boy, Joseph asked the elders the next question. "Is there an inn in the town where we can stay? I need to get my wife off the street as soon as I can, as you can plainly see."

Again, they were evasive. One admitted that his family kept an inn for travelers, but he knew for a fact that there was no room there. And so they all affirmed that it was the case in the whole town.

"Too many visitors this time of the year, you know," one confided.

The boy fumbled but finally got out the words "My parents, they are poor, shepherds, but they would let you stay with them for a small gift, I am sure. The place is small and mostly a cave that my family shares with our animals. My father does not go out anymore with the flocks. He was injured not so long ago defending our flock. Now it is my older brothers who spend the night in the fields."

Not having a choice, Joseph followed the boy to the edge of town. There the humble house of a shepherd sat, built into the hillside, obviously abutting a cave. One look at it made it clear that the house was not kosher. When Joseph had formerly lived in Bethlehem, he would have avoided this edge of the town for that very reason. The people there were regarded not as true Jews but as merely "people of the land," as the expression went. Joseph had struggled to overcome his prejudice and, in the end, accepted for his wife's sake an unoccupied space adjacent to that part of the cave where the family bedded their prize animals.

Unlike Joseph in his hesitation, the boy's mother, on seeing Mary's condition, sprang into action, sending Joseph into the other room. "No need for a man to be hanging around at a time like this," she chirped.

Despite Joseph's annoyance, the sound of the women clucking in the other room gave him comfort. They knew what they were doing, and they were bound to each other by a sisterhood of which he could not be a part.

The birth had come suddenly in the middle of the night. The mother and baby were well. Somehow the word had spread to the shepherds in the area, and they began to show up, even the boy's older brothers. Without warning, one of shepherds seized a lamb from the flock, gutted it on the spot, and set it roasting over an open fire. Out of the neighborhood, various dishes appeared, and even a skin or two of wine. A banquet fit for a king was spread on the open lawn in front of the little house! Joseph was surprised at how hungry he was, but even more at how hungry the women were who had assisted his wife. Their hunger, he would have bet, exceeded that of wolves, not to mention his own.

Within a day, Joseph was working with his hands. He had slipped out of the house, leaving his wife and child to sleep, in the early-morning light. He had noticed the night before that the shepherd's gate needed repairing. Without asking, he set to making it right. He then, at the shepherd's wife's bashful request, moved into the kitchen, repairing a bread trough, a spit, and a stool. The word spread. During the next week, neighbors began to ask for his services. Usually they paid Joseph with something that they had for barter.

It was toward the end of that week that he was suddenly aware that someone was standing behind him as he worked on the shutters of the neighboring house. The man had stood silently watching him for the longest time. His dress made it clear that he was not from this side of the village. Finally he spoke.

"Is it true that you are Joseph, the son of Jacob?"

"Yes," Joseph replied curtly.

The man said with a distinct edge in his voice, "Why have you come back to Bethlehem? Do you intend to stir up trouble again?"

"Who is it who is asking?"

"I am Jacob, your cousin, the son of Judah ben Matthan, your father's brother. It is I who now head David's family in Bethlehem."

"Ah," Joseph said, drawing out the word. "You did not know me when I needed help for my wife, but now you know me."

"Certainly you understand, Joseph, that the circumstance of your hasty departure from Bethlehem five years ago makes your sudden return suspicious to us. It took a good deal of work by us with the authorities to get things settled down after you left, and none of us want to go back to those times again."

Curbing his anger, Joseph replied, "Well, I am here with a wife and new son. I have no purpose other than securing for him his rightful name. I have no intention to start any trouble."

"The family will be greatly relieved to hear that," Jacob said. "We have taken counsel, and we are prepared to offer you a place to live. It is a small house, not in good repair, but it is yours, and we will help. It is now approaching the eighth day, and the child should be named and circumcised among his family."

Joseph swallowed his urge to bring up the repressive behavior of Herod's mercenaries, which he had publicly challenged when he was here before. He had very much wanted to ask his cousin what price the family had paid to get things settled down, but he refrained from doing so. Instead he said that the offer for the child's circumcision was most welcome.

When the eighth day came, Joseph, carrying the infant, led Mary across town, down the path from the shepherd's town to the gate, and from there up the road that led to Hebron, to a row of great houses that stretched along Bethlehem's west side. Not mansions so much as practical farmsteads, in the ancient style of the Israelites, built around a central courtyard. They were met at the gate to the courtyard, which was already full of people, mostly the women and children of the clan.

So the child was circumcised surrounded by the people of his ancestor Jesse, and his name was duly enrolled in the records of the town, Jesus, son of Joseph, son of David. The choice of the name Jesus raised questions. Jesus was not a family name, Joseph was told. But he was adamant, and so it was recorded Jesus.

When it was time to leave, Joseph led Mary around the corner of his cousin's home to an abandoned cottage built against its west wall. "Here is the home that the family has offered us," he said. "Over there is a well-watered terrace that will serve as a garden. To the west, about a hundred feet off, is a patch of pasture and a small field that goes with the house. I can make it into a home for us."

Realizing that Joseph was asking not only for her assent but also for reassurance, Mary expressed her delight.

As they returned to the other side of the town, he offered Mary the opinion that it must have been meant to be the way that it had come about. "Recall" he said to her, "that when Samuel came to Bethlehem to find the son of Jesse whom God had chosen to be the king of Israel, he was found not at the great house but rather among the sheepfolds where our own son has been born."

The Loss of Bethlehem a Second Time

Joseph had wasted no time in settling his wife, Mary, and their infant son in the little house provided by his family. It was, to be sure, small and run down, but the garden plot and modest pasture west of town boded well for its possibilities. The shepherd's daughter, who was about ten and who had been in on the birth, came to live with them. She doted on the child and was a great help to Mary. The shepherd's youngest son, the one Joseph had met in the gate, showed up daily to work as a day laborer for Joseph. Joseph in turn taught the boy his trade and believed that he would do much for the shepherd town that had taken them in when no one else would. It was not by any means a full restitution of the property Joseph had left behind when he had been forced to flee Bethlehem, but it provided a living for his family, and it satisfied him. The clan in turn was pleased to see the ruin returned to prosperity and their numbers augmented, especially given that his little one was a boy.

Joseph continued to be very disciplined in his commitment not to start trouble. The only rub with the family was that from time to time the women from the other side of town came to visit the child they had delivered. Clearly they had established a close bond with Mary and she with them. And from time to time, Joseph went to the other side of town and did things as a carpenter for those who were called the people of the land.

That had not, however, stopped the extended family of Bethlehemites from embracing his charming young wife and his handsome son. Joseph even began again to study Torah, and he was called to read from time to time in the village's synagogue. The dream was happening.

That is, until a strange and unexpected event intervened to change their lives yet again. As usual, it was the kids running in the street who had brought the news that something was about to happen. A strange retinue of travelers had arrived in the town. The dress of the leading men made it clear that they were foreigners of some special standing. Not kings or priests but, as they had announced, "men devoted to wisdom." It was flattering for the town to be visited by such a retinue. Their inquires led them to the house of Joseph and Mary. The townspeople looked on as the men talked with Joseph. He took them into the house, where they praised the child and gave him elaborate gifts. The townspeople, including the family, sensed that this auspicious visit would place Bethlehem on the map and that somehow they themselves might benefit from this stroke of fortune.

The retinue of these distinguished visitors, who had waited in the yard, could not refrain from impressing the gathering of extended family and neighbors. They bragged about their recent reception at the palace of King Herod. Indeed, they boasted that they had been invited to return to his court after they had completed their mission. They could hardly wait to return to the king's lavish hospitality. Everyone was most impressed by this and imagined themselves being guests at the palace.

When evening came, Joseph was once again suddenly aware of his cousin's presence. It was Jacob who began, "I regret to say this, but this is not good."

"I behaved in a most respectful way," Joseph replied defensively.

"It is the notice. It is not good in our view to be noticed. The Herodians are bound to poke their noses into this sooner or later."

"They were just curious old men. That's all they were. They meant no one harm—I promise you."

Joseph rebutted his cousin's allegations, but at the same time, he knew that he himself had been uneasy about the visit well before his cousin had come. That night, he watched Mary play with the child, coaxing steps out of him. Then they lay down to sleep, where sleep had been so pleasant for the last several months. Soon he was aware that Mary was sleeping soundly but that for him it was going to be one of those difficult nights when sleep would come only in fits and starts.

When it came, it was filled with dread and struggle. Somewhere in the struggle, a voice was saying ever more clearly, "You must leave Bethlehem immediately for the life of the child is at risk." He lay there in the dark realizing that his heart was racing and that he was covered in sweat. The implausible destination of Egypt that the voice had designated for his flight seemed preposterous. The great ancestor for whom he was named had gone into Egypt, it was true. But he had gone not by choice but as a prisoner and a slave. Indeed, the Torah forbade it, for it was written in the scroll of Genesis, "You shall not return to Egypt." He swore to himself that he would not go into Egypt as long as he was free.

While he had doubts about the truth of the voice he heard in his half sleep, he was so full of dread that he could not but act on its advice. He shook his poor wife awake in the middle of the night. He knew that his frenzy was terrifying her as she speechlessly followed his instructions. There was in his mind no other way. When he tried to explain to Mary why they needed to leave immediately, it made no sense to her. The idea of being uprooted again troubled her. Joseph was sensitive to her pain and tried to be patient. Reluctantly, and with the vague promise that it might be nothing more than spending a few days away in Hebron, Mary yielded to his plan. And so quietly in the dark of night they slipped out of Bethlehem without telling anyone and took the road south, down the spine of the hill country, to Hebron.

Hebron, Joseph told Mary as they walked along, was also a town that belonged to the tribe of Judah, and from it, David had reigned over Judah for ten years before the other tribes called him to be their king as well. They could come to feel at home there as much as they had in Bethlehem. At any rate, he assured her, as soon as things had blown over in Bethlehem, they could return. There was really nothing to fear. He tried very hard to convince her, without being able to convince himself, that the trip to Hebron was merely a temporary precaution and that there was nothing to fear.

A Stop among the Oaks of Mamre

Joseph had gambled away a modest future in Nazareth in the hope of a much greater future in Bethlehem. Indeed, it had started to pay off. It had grown as in a dream. It had not been long before he no longer needed to use his hands to make a living and he actually began again to take up the study of Torah. His young son, Jesus, for whom he had gained the right to be enrolled in the census of Bethlehem as a son of David, grew daily in wisdom and in favor among his peers. Then, quite as suddenly, the dream had been snatched away by an odd and unexpected event for which he was in no way to blame. A group of travelers had sought out his son, claiming to have seen signs about his birth in the heavens. Inadvertently they had exposed him and his family to the Herodian court, forcing him to leave Bethlehem in great haste. Now the only future he had left lay with the little child.

He once again was a sojourner in the land, walking with his wife and child and their donkey loaded with their belongings; the tools of his trade, which he would have to resume; and the few other personal things that they could carry. Underneath that were hidden the gifts as much to keep them from his own sight as from that of a potential thief. They were, after all, the cause of this flight. The thought that he would still be in Bethlehem had these gift bearers not signaled to the world his presence there was like gall on his tongue.

In the dark of the night, he had led the little party of his wife, child, and beast of burden up onto the ridge road that went down the spine of the hill country to Hebron. The Herodium, that hateful conical fortress that Herod had built on the edge of Bethlehem, that marred the pastoral landscape of Bethlehem and stood as an obscene reminder of Herod's rule, disappeared over his left shoulder. The distance that they needed to cover that first day was little more than fourteen miles, but it was uphill all the way. Hebron sat at the top of the ridge at the highest point of all Judea, which, it occurred to him, was one of the reasons why his ancestor David had made it his first capital. For all that, the walk had not been hard, and already on the horizon stood a clump of oak trees, which by Joseph's calculations would be the oaks of Mamre.

Among those oaks, Abraham had camped, fed angels, received the promise of a son, and closed his wife's eyes for the last time.

"Father Abraham," he had heard himself asking, "why is it that our God allows men to make other men wander the face of the earth?"

The question began to repeat itself in Joseph's head in rhythm with his feet as they lifted the child who was riding on his back a step higher and closer to the oaks.

Upon arriving at the oaks, he swung the boy down, who quickly scampered about examining the crop of acorns strewn on the ground. He then lifted the load off the donkey's back. He took a great cloth from the load and spread it for his young wife so that she could take rest. Mary smiled at him, and he attempted to smile back. After everything was in order for the others, Joseph sat down and let his head sink into his hands.

His fingers pressed hard on his eyes, bringing both dark and flashes of false light. The tired that he felt in his body was both physical and mental. Why was this happening to him? Had God or fate singled him out to never have any peace?

"Why not to you?" he seemed to have heard a voice return like an echo. "Are you more blessed than I, who did not have a son, who then, out of time, was given a son only to be asked to sacrifice that son?"

A pause let the full force of the question fall into the depths of Joseph's thoughts.

"Are you any more cursed than I, who journeyed the whole of my life never having a home once I left Ur in obedience to the call of my God?"

A verse from a psalm came then to Joseph's mind. "Hear my prayer, O Lord, and give ear to my cry; hold not your peace at my tears. For I am but a sojourner with you, a wayfarer, as all my forebears were."

"Yes, Father Abraham," the reply formed in his head. "I am like you and your son and your son's son, but can't that ever come to an end for us?"

Then abruptly his mind jumped to the beginning of that psalm that he had often sung in synagogue: "I will put a muzzle on my mouth!"

As he began to come out of the circle of his thoughts, he could feel the intense prayers of his wife for him. "Mary," he said softly, "make us three cakes, something a little special, to celebrate, and I will go fetch us milk and curds." He smiled at the thought and then explained to her, "Here, in this very place, our father Abraham once entertained angels and received the great promise of God. You know he was a sojourner all of his life, and like me, he did not expect to have a son but was given one by God. And you, Mary, you are as beautiful as Sarah, and if we were to go so far as our father Abraham into Egypt, God forbid, I should have to tell them like Abraham did about Sarah, that you are my sister, or they would try to bump me off!"

She poked him with her tiny fist, laughed, and then blushed deeply.

Joseph, smiling, went off to buy some fresh milk for them from a nearby shepherd. In no time at all, they were feasting under the oaks of Mamre on fine cakes and curd in the company of the angels.

Under a Broom Tree near Beersheba

At first it seemed that Joseph had been right about Hebron. He and his family were quickly welcomed by the people of Hebron, and they felt very much at home. They had visited the Haran el Khali, the great complex that Herod had built over the graves of Sarah and Abraham, and felt themselves profoundly privileged to have done so. Joseph soon found work as a carpenter and was respected as son of David. Mary had quickly made women friends from whom she received reassuring advice about how to raise a child. Jesus had found a world filled with intriguing places to explore on his toddler legs.

Before a month had run its course, however, the family paid Joseph a visit. Joseph was bent over a doorsill that was in need repair, when, as before, a presence interrupted him. Looking up, he saw his cousin Jacob, who was head of the David family in Bethlehem.

"We were rather certain that this was where you would head," Jacob said.

"How are things in Bethlehem?" Joseph replied tersely.

"Very tense!" was the equally curt answer. "Herod's officers are asking questions."

"About what?"

"About whether there had been any strange visitors to our town during the past year. As far as we know, no one has said anything to them. But they won't stop. Sooner or later, someone will let it out."

"Yes, I understand. That is why I left," Joseph said wearily. "You know that I did everything I could to avoid being noticed by the authorities."

"We will give you that," Jacob said grudgingly. "But as it turned out, that isn't enough. They will hold the whole town responsible. You know how they are," he added sourly.

"What would you have me do?" Joseph asked in frustration.

"When it comes out, the only way that we will have to save the town from trouble is to tell them where you are."

"I see."

Nothing more was said. The cousin rejoined a group of young men who had accompanied him to Hebron, and they went through the motions of going to the Haran el Khali to venerate their ancestors' graves, as if the sole purpose of the trip had been this pilgrimage. Joseph finished the repair of the doorsill without any sign of haste, received his pay, and then walked slowly back to the lodging where he was staying with Mary and the child. As he went, he was thinking out how he was going to explain to her why their time had run out at Hebron.

The next morning, they were on the road that runs down the wadi of the Besor, the waterway that drained Judea's Shephelah into the Mediterranean. Their goal was the settlement of Beersheba, which lay some fifteen miles farther southwest of Hebron. It was a well-traveled route, though not like the traffic-laden way down the Jordan valley, on which they had once traveled from Nazareth to Bethlehem. This was Jerusalem's route into Egypt. In Joseph's darkest night thoughts, the nagging insistence that he must take his family into Egypt had continued to reoccur. But in his day thoughts, and especially those that he shared with Mary, he never, except as a joke, ventured to speak of going into Egypt. Just being on this stretch of road, however, made Joseph feel uneasy, as if something were causing him to take his family into Egypt in spite of his determination not to.

On the road, he felt the shade of the patriarch Isaac coming toward him, hastily returning from Egypt, where he had disgraced himself for fear of his life. Between the pressures of population, which had set his father, Abraham, on his journey westward, and enmity of Abimelech, the king of Egypt from whom he was now fleeing, he had found this barren stretch of land a reasonable space for his family to settle. Here he had dug a well, only to have Abimelech contest it. But after a confrontation, and a solemn oath sworn at the well, Abimelech withdrew, and Isaac never returned to Egypt. The oath had held, and Beersheba had remained to this day an outpost of Israel on the border of Egypt. Could he find room for his family in Beersheba, and could the oath not to go into Egypt hold for him as well?

As the midpoint of the day passed, he became aware of a shadow in the road that followed him. Not only was it lengthening, but it was also growing in weight. His feet seemed to drag as the miles went on. Indeed, he was not the only fugitive to walk this road. Elijah had walked this road to Beersheba heavy with despair. He had in his zeal done what he had thought that God had asked him to do, but as a result, he had become a fugitive from his king.

In the wilderness near to Beersheba, he had found a solitary broom tree, where he had sat down to die.

It was time for a stop, and the only refuge from the sun was a broom tree that grew in a parched wadi. Joseph seated his family in its sparse shade and brought out of his sack a ring of dried figs and some nuts. He tore the figs off the ring and meticulously cut them into small pieces for his son. He watched with satisfaction as the young Jesus mixed the sweetness of a morsel of fig with the sturdiness of the nut's meat. A bright lad, he thought.

Before him his own portion remained uneaten. He had prepared the meal for his wife and his son out of duty. But for him to take his own portion required an act of will that was not forthcoming. He let the sun sink into this flesh to ease its weariness, which seemed to be unto death. Dreamily he looked across the road at another family who had stopped to eat and rest. They were a husband, a wife, three sons, and two daughters ranging in age from two to perhaps eighteen. A formidable family, he thought. When Mary was drawing water from the well before their lunch, she had talked to the woman. They were coming from the city On, which was located in Egypt, not far from the border. Mary explained to Joseph that the family had lived in On for some time. The woman had told her that she had really liked there. In that city, there was a great and powerful synagogue. There was lots of money floating around. Their own people there were very rich. But in the end, they did not like the lifestyle, so they had decided to return to their village just outside Jerusalem. Mary, in her domesticity, felt the wife's regret at losing her home there. Joseph, in a more worldly way, silently speculated about what kind of trouble the husband might have gotten himself into in that very commercial city of On that put him on the road again. Then Joseph saw them in another light. He simply saw them as another family on the move, displaced by the machinations of commerce or politics, hoping that somehow their next place would be different. They were legions, these displaced families of the earth, roaming the roads of the world. He, his wife, and their young son were one of the army of wanderers.

"Why, God, do you allow it to happen? Why are we part of them?" he had asked.

The answer returned, "In order that I might be part of them," in a way that left no room for questioning.

Accepting that answer, Joseph looked to see if he could see where God was a part of this fearful and apparently endless migration of people. And what he saw was himself, his wife, and his son.

"Lord, we are part of it. I, the least of your servants, reluctantly, my beautiful wife Mary anxiously, and the child whom you have placed into my care innocently. We are part of these sojourners, but—forgive me for asking—where are you?"

"Do you yet not see how I live in the child?" came a voice deep in the dark of his mind. "Get up and eat, or the journey will be too much for you."

So he arose and ate hastily what he had formerly ignored and felt his strength return, so much so that he supposed that he could go forty days and forty nights on the power of that food alone and nothing more. Then, gathering his wife and his son, he set them back on their journey, arriving in Beersheba in the late afternoon.

Beersheba, at that time, was a settlement of scattered households, smaller than Hebron, even smaller than Bethlehem or Nazareth. It was a dry and dusty oasis in the heart of the Negev desert. If it had once had its day, the only reason for it to have existed today was as a stopping place on the road between Israel and Egypt. It offered Joseph and his family little except that it was the farthest point that they could go and still be in Israel, the leaving of which Joseph had not yet accepted despite the voice in his head that kept speaking to him of Egypt.

Once again they began the process of settling into a community, seeking shelter, work, and those associations necessary to survive. By now, he and his wife had become rather masterful at what it took to do this. Joseph sought solace in the fact that it was at Beersheba great father Isaac had chosen to sojourn, and it was there that he had established an altar for the worship of the God of his father, Abraham. If God had been a shield for Isaac in Beersheba, would he not be a shield for his little family?

The Sycamore at the Edge of Egypt

The town of Beersheba made a practice of knowing little about what went on in the rest of Judea, or the world, for that matter. The people there seemed to like it that way. They did not ask questions such as "What made you decide to come to Beersheba?" or even "Where are you from?" The assumption was that either you would soon move on, which made such information irrelevant, or for those who did stay for any length of time, such information was better not known. In fact, this preference for not knowing gave Beersheba a particular edge in its discovered purpose as a way station for those who trafficked in sundry things between Egypt and Jerusalem. If it were possible for someone to remain hidden in Israel, it would most likely be in Beersheba. That provided Joseph with the hope that his travels could stop here.

Indeed, no one from the family had visited Joseph while they were in Beersheba. There were no officers in King Herod's service poking around. Beersheba lived outside the realm, fulfilling its purpose as a point of passage for travelers passing through the desert with no questions asked. No one had in fact in the course of the last couple of months bothered to ask Joseph where he had come from or why he was there with his family. The general procedure in Beersheba was don't ask and don't tell. After their disappointment in Hebron, he was relieved that this was the way things were.

What had finally changed this world for Joseph was a chance overhearing of a group of travelers who had come from Jerusalem. They seemed unable to keep from talking about a story they claimed they had witnessed. No one in Beersheba listened to them, but they just compulsively chewed on the story among themselves, reassuring themselves that they really had witnessed what they said they had seen. Joseph had not yet fully acquired the skill of not listening. So words like "Bethlehem," "grim," and "insane tyrant" penetrated his ears. These travelers claimed that King Herod had ordered his soldiers to seize all the children in Bethlehem under two years of age and to kill them. Dozens of children had died before their parents' eyes. They themselves had passed through town only days afterward and had witnessed the fresh graves and had heard the heartrending cries of mothers whose children were no more.

The terror of what they described was unimaginable to Joseph. As much as he hated the Herodians, this action seemed to go beyond anything he could possibly have imagined. Unlike the people of the village, who ignored the babbling as if it had nothing to do with them, Joseph had challenged the report. How did they know that this story was true? They had passed through Bethlehem on their way south shortly after it had happened. When he had questioned them about Bethlehem, they described the village to him in a way that forced him to believe they had been there. They had even claimed to have seen the graves in a place precisely where the village buried their dead.

Grudgingly, he had accepted the truth. Up to that time, he had never entertained the idea that it wasn't him Herod sought to destroy. Now it was vividly clear that Herod was not concerned about him, but wanted to kill his son, this innocent child with no home. *God, what is wrong with the world?* Joseph cried in his shaken mind.

After the indignation of disbelief came a crushing wave of guilt. *It is my fault*, he had thought. If I had not insisted on bringing my wife to Bethlehem to give birth to the boy, then dozens of children in Bethlehem would not be dead!

The illogic of this guilt did not escape him. He and this child for whom he had been made guardian were victims along with the dead children and their families. In spite of the logic, the guilt that flooded his mind would not abate.

Why, God, should victims feel guilt and he who ordered the crime and those who executed it feel none? As Joseph thought about it and tried to imagine returning to Bethlehem or anywhere else in Judea at some future time, he came to the stark conclusion that such a return would be utterly impossible. The only relief he would find from his guilt would be to be as far away from his countrymen as he possibly could be. The thought of going down into Egypt, which he had long resisted, was the only answer. The voice in his dreams, nightmares, had been saying that to him all along, and now it could no longer be resisted.

He had gone to Mary to tell her that it was necessary for them to take up their journey again.

"Where to?" Mary asked.

"To Egypt?" he replied.

"Oh no," she sighed. "It is not that we are leaving anything here, but if we go into Egypt, will we ever return? Will we ever have a real home?"

The same doubts had gone through Joseph's mind as well, but he could not bear to leave his young wife with such doubts. He said to her, "Abraham, you know, went into Egypt and came back. And Joseph, the son of Jacob, did so, and eventually the whole family of Jacob had gone into Egypt, and God called them back. Jacob had himself stayed in Beersheba, and God had spoken to him in the night and said, 'I am God, the God of your father; do not be afraid to go down to Egypt.' I think he is saying the same to us.

"When it is time, God will call your son out of Egypt, and we shall bring him to his own country."

The remark comforted Mary and himself as well. But Mary had to add, in what was close to a whisper, "In the latter case, that took four hundred years!"

They were back on the road that followed the wadi of Besor, which just past Beersheba turned westward to the sea. It took them to Shahen, which had once belonged to the tribe of Simeon. There the sometime river left the hill country and flowed across the coastal plain. On the plain, the valley intersected the road to Egypt that passed on to Raphia on the coast and then took the long the curve of the Great Sea, ending in a run due west. On the third day after leaving Beersheba, they came upon the east edge of the city of On, which the Greeks called the city of Heliopolis, the city of the sun. It was in this ancient city that the son of Jacob, Joseph, had chosen a bride, Asenath, a daughter of the priest of On.

In its streets could be heard Greek and Coptic, and even their own native Aramaic, because a large Jewish population had remained there. They prospered as merchants and kept a large synagogue that proudly called itself the house of Onias. Not far from the synagogue was a park, and there under a great sycamore tree Joseph had chosen to stop to give his family a rest and to calculate how they might make On their home. The child, who was ever more adventurous, had been allowed to explore, and at a place where the land sharply rose onto hill. The boy had caused a pile of rocks to tumble downward. Both Joseph and Mary, snapping out of their preoccupations, raced to the place where the boy was, only to find a spring of water flowing out of the breach made by the missing rocks. After each of them had enjoyed a deep draft of the cold fresh water, Mary set to work washing their clothes. Townspeople were soon on the scene marveling at the flow of such fine water. Realizing what a valuable resource this spring would be, they graciously welcomed the young family to their town.

Deeper into Egypt

On was a cosmopolitan city. Its citizens boasted that Plato, the founder of Greek philosophy, had spent his youth in their city and that Moses, the head of Israel's prophesy, had been raised there. In the city, a large and affluent Jewish population had continued to live over centuries. It was clear that Joseph could find both security and prosperity for his family in On. But that was not what he was looking for. What was it he was looking for? His answer to that question was a little vague in his own mind. It was not so much a place for the family to build a future as a place for them to buy some time. Moreover, he personally needed a place that did not constantly remind him of the awful murder of children in Bethlehem for which he could not help feeling responsible for in some way. The Jewish community in On was ready to share their prosperity with Joseph, but on the other hand, they approved the worldliness of the Herodians. They were quite willing to dismiss the excesses of Herod in favor of the fundamental prosperity that his government brought Jews everywhere. This was quite difficult for Joseph to accept. How they could discount the stories like the one about the killing of babies, or justify the corruption and violence of Herod's partisans, was beyond him. Should not the guilt that he felt be theirs as well to some degree?

So it was not long before he and his wife, Mary, were speaking about moving on. First, they moved deeper into the city to the part called Cairo, finding a neighborhood at the head of the Nile with a small synagogue. It was a neighborhood where the grand things of state and commerce seldom came up. This was a much more conducive place for Joseph and his need to avoid his feeling of guilt, which came over him from time to time like the breakers of the sea.

But their comfort with the quieter neighborhood did not last long either. They had been traveling from place to place for so long, a couple of years now, that they had lost the habit of settling down. When Joseph did some carpentry on a boat due to sail down the Nile, the captain offered to take him along so that he could continue to work on his boat. After wrestling with the idea of yet another move, he broached the topic with Mary. Mary understood by now how Joseph struggled with his guilt and knew that the demands of a move would take his mind off the thoughts that occasioned bouts of guilt. After pondering the possibility with him for a couple of days, she gave her consent. Far up the Nile, some 150 miles from Cairo, there was yet another small Jewish community in a place called Qusquam. It sat at the bend in the Nile just before the river entered the fabled Valley of the Kings. Perhaps it was here that they could find a fresh start.

The slow days on the river had a kind of idyllic feel, as if on the river they were somehow detached from the world itself. The child who was now approaching four had a precocious interest in the details of the river, which was unlike anything he had ever experienced before. Having traveled for a couple of weeks, they were taken eastward by the Nile, and there was the small but bustling farm village of Deir Al Garnous. It was the captain's intention to take on a load of wheat in the village and then return to Cairo. Liking the feel of the village, Joseph decided with Mary's consent to leave the boat and settle in the village. The captain had tried to persuade Joseph to return with him for he enjoyed Joseph's company and valued his work. When Joseph had politely declined, the captain wished them well and spoke of seeing them some months hence on a return voyage. From there, Joseph and Mary traveled away from the river a short distance to the hill known locally as Bird Mountain. There they found a cave in which they could make a home. It was not in fact far from the village of Qusquam. There they were greeted by a small Jewish community that had been there for many years. It seemed to Joseph that he was at last far enough away from everything to find peace.

Joseph relished the relief of living on the edge of the world, where Herod was unknown and where he enjoyed watching the child at play with the children of the community. In a place so far away that very likely God himself would forget about them. If God had had a special purpose of the child, why would he have allowed him to be banished to the ends of the earth, where civilization lapsed in the dark continent, anyway?

Yet seeing Jesus's interaction with the children of Qusquam, the boy's obvious and effortless concern for them, Joseph realized that if anyone anywhere else was to be saved, it would also entail saving these children. If that were true, then why couldn't it in fact begin right here?

Six months passed, which was the longest time that they had been settled anywhere since they had left Bethlehem. The life was so simple and so uncomplicated that Joseph began to wish that it would never end. It felt to him like a second Bethlehem! The idea of returning to Judea was fraught with such problems for him that it was quite unthinkable.

Then he awoke one morning and the first thought in his head was that Herod was dead. Where had that come from? How could he be so certain? He reflected on the voice in the night that had troubled his sleep and recovered a phrase: "Those who sought the young child's life are dead." He closed his eyes tighter against the growing light of the new day, and then he remembered other words: "Arise. Take the young child and his mother and go to the land of Israel." He lay inactive in his bed for yet another stretch of time as if preparing a script in his mind. Then he literally bounded out of bed. He went straight to Mary and bent over her and said gently, "It is time."

"Time to get up? The light is just breaking," she replied sleepily.

"Time"—a smile came across his face— "to go back home to Israel."

Mary paused. "How do you know? How can you be certain?"

Now it was time for Joseph to pause. After some time, he said, "I just feel it so deeply in my head that I can't doubt it."

"Well," Mary said, getting up and beginning to assemble things for the trip, "it is a long way."

"Yes. But it will go by quickly, I think."

Her voice still resonating with doubt, Mary asked, "When we get there, where will we go?"

With an uncharacteristic lightheartedness, Joseph replied, "We will have to see when we get there, I guess."

And both began to imagine something like home and in each case the beginning of a normal family life in which they could let the special little family that they had become expand.

Within a week, the captain had returned and rejoiced to have them as passengers on the return to Cairo. Their friends in Qusquam were grieved but happy for them also. They said to Joseph and Mary, "You have brought something special to us that will never really leave us. We feel like we are a second Bethlehem and that you will always be a part of us. For us, Mary has become and will always remain our El-Adawiya—that is to say God's friend."

The Return to Cairo

The boat laden with grain worked its way down the Nile with little effort. While there were the usual repairs for Joseph to occupy himself with, there was much spare time. In fact, his old friend the boat's pilot seemed more desirous of conversation than getting work out of him. Joseph, who had long forgone talking politics, was delighted to catch up. How was Egypt managing under the Romans? The pilot was all too pleased to ventilate his opinion about the Romans. They were easy enough for a man with some brains to work around. Of course, what they did was to find among the local population a body of retainers. In turn, for their collusion, they were enriched and given privileges by their overlords. These retainers were styled as kings and queens, nobles, literati, and so on. An honest man did his best to avoid them for they were so anxious about their status that they were more dangerous than the Romans themselves. The pilot continued, "The Romans are harsh, but these lackeys will sell you out for copper penny!"

"Ah," Joseph said, "like our Herodians back home!"

Brightening by this shift in the topic, the pilot asked him, "Have you heard how your Herodians have fared?"

"No," Joseph replied. "What was so wonderful about Qusquam was there was no news about the outside world. Of course, the world didn't know anything about Qusquam, but that seemed like a small price to pay for that privilege."

"Well, you might be interested to know that Herod's brood has not done so well. The Romans decided that no one would replace him as king. They divided the territory into four regions, giving each of the four sons a region to rule—if that is the right word to describe what such lackeys do."

"Better," Joseph said, "to front for the Romans and skim off the cream!"

"The oldest son, Archelaus, was made tetrarch—what nice ring that has—of Judea but lost his job in a couple of years. He got too big for his britches, I think, and was sent packing. Herod Antipas, the buffoon, was given Galilee and Perea. He seems to have suited the Romans' best. Philip was given Ituraea and Trachonitis. Abilene was given to someone named Lysanias.

"So it seems," Joseph said, "the Romans themselves have taken control over Judea, eliminating the middlemen."

There were a number of stops along the way and renewed conversation. As they neared the end of the journey, the river slowed, and sun burned brighter. The crew suddenly became busier navigating the delta, so Joseph found himself in the bow of the boat with his family, watching the scenery. He had begun to drift off, having the strange sensation that the boat around him had contracted till he felt that he was bobbing on the water in little more than a shell. All he saw from this almost submerged position was water all around him rising and falling, giving off stabbing flashes of light. He was all but asleep when he heard the boy's voice ask, "Joseph, is it here that Moses was found floating in a basket?"

"Funny you should ask that," Joseph replied to Jesus. "I was just dreaming that I was floating on the river in a basket, just like a baby!"

Jesus snorted at the thought.

"Yes," Joseph continued, "I think this could very well be the place where Moses was found floating in a basket."

Joseph watched Jesus deep in thought, wondering what he would come up with.

"We are like Moses, aren't we?" Jesus said. "We have been in Egypt, and now we are leaving to return to our own land."

"Yes, much like Moses, I think," Joseph said.

Jesus provided a summation: "It has been good for us to have been in Egypt."

And the family slipped back into silence.

Soon they had landed and took leave of their friend who had piloted the boat. They found themselves among the old neighbor where they had lived for a short while. They stayed the night and caught up with their old neighbor and had tried to explain what a magical place Qusquam had been, but they could tell that their old neighbor could not imagine why anyone would visit a place so far off, let alone stay there. The next day, they traveled to On and found the spring that Jesus had discovered still flowing and the people still remembering how the little child had discovered it. How they marveled that little boy had grown so tall and fair!

An old neighbor insisted that the family spend the night with them, as much time as they would like, in fact. Mary and Joseph consented and found themselves being entertained that evening at supper with many of the neighbors. Each took time to try to talk them out of returning to Israel. What more did a Jew need than what he could find at the splendid synagogue of On? Did you need high priests devoted to intrigue? So-called kings? The foot of the Roman on your neck? Or the arrogance of the Jerusalemites who thought all other Jews were somehow inferior?

"Yes, yes, all that is so," Joseph said, "but it is home."

"Our work is there," the boy of six had added, having managed to stay at the men's table through the whole discussion.

ZECHARIAH IN SILENCE

In the season of his silence,
      he watched his wife grow large with child,
      the child they had come to think could never be.
      He thought he had never seen such joy
      riding on the waves of fear and pain,
      nor had he ever felt such churning in his brain.

      Perhaps, he reasoned, it was simply that a thought
      falls back on itself when it lacks a tongue to speak it.
      How much he wished now to speak to her of his love
      and bring to her some calm, some quiet, or some balm
      to her fears and to her pain and to the churning of his brain.

In the season of his silence,
      he received a steady stream of visitors
      who came to bring him good cheer,
      and not few, it seemed to him, to peer
      into the future changed by the coming of this child,
      upsetting their calculation of who would be his heir.

      Ah, it was, he thought, as the psalmist once said.
      They come to see me and speak empty words.
      In their hearts they collect false rumors
      that they will take and spread abroad.
      It galled him most, however,
      when they chattered on about angels,
      when it was utterly clear they had no clue
      what it was like to hear an angel speak.
      Then he had wanted in the worst way to say,
      "Angels, you fools, are quite terrifying—
      their very beauty brings on fear and trembling,
      above all the alarm of new beginnings
      in what one had come to think of as safely ending.

In the season of his silence,
    he imagined the troubled years to come,
    when he and his wife would be gone
    and the child yet young would fall into the hands
    of others whose present promises he could not trust.
    This child shall never be a priest like me, he thought,
    offerings incense as I on the altar in the Holy of Holies.
    They will find way to send him off
    into a wilderness to be lost.
    But there, he thought, there
    that boy would find a voice,
    and to their surprise he would return a prophet.

More than anything, it was the name
    that roiled his brain. "How John?"
    Priests of Zechariah's course had never been
    called by such a common name as that,
    which would link him with the common folk.
    Yet at the breaking of his silence,
    when his tongue was at last undone,
    he blurted out, "His name is John."
    And then, rising up, he had sung,
    "Blessed is the God of Israel
    for he has come to his people to set them free …"

FROM QUMRAN TO THE RIVER

The discoveries at Qumran have had a number of impacts on New Testament studies. The idea that John the Baptist was influenced by the Qumran community has had a lasting impact even though there is no way to confirm or deny it. It is, however, possible to test the plausibility of the hypothesis by attempting to imagine how one could move from the sanctuary of Qumran to a mission of baptizing along the Jordan River. The poetic cycle that follows is an exercise in imagination. It does not claim that this is the way it happened; it suggests only that it could have happened. At the same time, the study makes clear just how different John the Baptist was from the masters of Qumran and the Essenes in general.

I
A Boy in the Scriptorium

The masters of Qumran had taken their seats
 for the common meal at the end of their week.
 The boys of the order, those who had excelled,
 were allowed to stand in the hall, to serve
 and observe what they themselves could be.
 A sensation of sorts passed through the room,
 when the one who was famous, but seldom seen,
 had come out of retreat and taken his seat,
 the one they called the Master of the Cave.

The orphaned boy, apprenticed to the scriptorium,
 had himself observed this master depart across the broad field
 where the dead of order were buried, an army in waiting,
 and then climb the steep palisade of the wilderness
 until, like a crow, he had become a black spot,
 ducking and weaving its way up, and finally had disappeared
 into the dark of the mouth of one of the innumerable caves.

When the evening had ended, the boy intersected that master
 and kneeling before him had breathlessly asked
 what it was that he contemplated in the cave.

"Contemplated?" the master replied. "You know that word?"
The boy had used an unusual Hebrew word,
so he said with a gulp, "I heard it in the scroll of Habakkuk."
"Good for you," said the master. "What I contemplated was silence."
Silence was never heard, the boy thought, in the scriptorium,
a place where words were endlessly rehearsed, copied, and declaimed.
It occurred to him that his fellows in the scriptorium would think the reply funny,
for they probably never heard the silence of which the master spoke.
Though he thought that he had, long ago, with his father,
in the time that they sat together before his father had died,
albeit the boy was almost too young to remember,
but somehow did, despite all that time that had passed.

The next day in the scriptorium, as the work of the day was ending,
    he had dared to speak to his master, the Master of Texts,
    and ask him if it might ever be possible for him
    to visit a cave like the one in which the other master lived.
    His master had replied to him brusquely,
    "There are too many words here to be tended
    and memorized for you to take such time."
    And then sharply asked, "Have you finished Habakkuk?"
    The boy paused and said, "Almost."
    And bargained on, "If I could by tomorrow,
    would I have your leave for the remaining days of the week
    to visit one of the caves up on the edge of the wilderness?"
    The Master of the Text, thinking this to be an idle boast,
    and a good way to humiliate the boy, said, "If ..."

The following morning, the boy stood before the Master of Texts,
    and Habakkuk flowed from his lips like a crystal stream.
    The master had no choice but to let him go,
    so shortly the boy was on his way past the field of the dead,
    onto the cliffs, yellow in the morning sun,
    nimbly scampering ever higher.
    The thought occurred to him that he was being watched
    and that by now he must look like a crow flitting about.
    Just above lay the darkness, and he relished the thought
    that in a moment he would disappear into it, and then what?
    The silence, which he remembered from past,
    would again be his, and if it was, then what?
    Was that the way text ended?
    Or was it the way text found itself?

The Boy and the Cave

The boy from the scriptorium returned to his place of work
      after the days that he had spent in the cave high up on the cliff.
      The Master of Text greeted him tersely and acidly asked
      if he had enjoyed his time off, and without waiting for a reply,
      he went on to assign him a task larger than usual,
      a sign to the boy that he should not ever hope to do so again.
      Still his hope survived, and a few nights later,
      as the boy walked out of the hall after the common meal,
      he found his way blocked by the Master of the Cave,
      who quietly asked him what he had contemplated in the cave.
      "Silence," he had haltingly replied.
      "Good," said the master warmly, and added,
      "Once you have heard it, you will return to it."

The time that had passed since then, four years, if he reckoned it right,
      had allowed him only a few returns to the cave on the cliff.
      But the Master of the Cave had been right about the silence—
      whether in the cave or not, he had returned to it.
      In some sense, he reflected, there was
      a battle in their order between text and cave
      that was being fought over or through him.
      Now he, the boy, had become a man.
      He had come to the end of his apprenticeship
      and to his admission to the scriptorium as one of its fellows.
      The Master of the Text commended him
      as the head of his class,
      as a son of priests,
      as the very kind that the order most coveted.
      In other words, the boy could see,
      he had become a feather in his master's hat.

To his great surprise, the Master of the Text asked him
      if there was anything that he needed in order to better prepare
      for the awesome installation whose date had now been set.
      "Nothing," he had hastily replied, but then he had added,
      wishfully, or perhaps it was resentfully, he couldn't be sure,
      "A time for contemplation in the cave up on the cliff."
      To his surprise, the Master of the Text had said yes.

So on the next morning, his heart light,
he bundled a few things in a knapsack
and set out on the climb up the cliffs,
yellow in the morning sun.
Having reached the great height
over the floor of the rift in which the order's foundation sat,
he thought of those below who might be watching from there his ascent.
By now, he would look to them like a crow, flitting from ledge to ledge,
which, he thought, was no mind to him, except perhaps that one might be a boy.
He moved over the last of the ledges, toward the black at the mouth of a cave.
He stepped into it, disappearing to those who were watching below,
and he hoped that they would be convinced by the show.
In reality, he slipped through the black onto a path that led
into the silence of the wilderness beyond
in order that he might become John.

III
The Young Man in the Wilderness

Stepping out on the wilderness of Judea,
      high over the valley in which he had lived half his life,
      the man was resolved to begin a new life,
      only too aware of how unprepared he was.
      Wandering rather aimlessly in this big new world,
      he came upon a group of shepherds,
      who upon seeing him appeared to be much amused.
      Trying to adjust his overtrained speech,
      he asked for their help, to which they
      replied with a question of their own:
      "Have you ever begged from an Essene master?"
      Puzzled by their question, he had finally stammered a no.
      "Don't. It isn't worth it"—which heightened their levity.
      Suddenly aware of how strange he must appear to these rustics,
      dressed, as he was, in the white tunic of an Essene, on their turf,
      he had laughed with them and then dared to go on to explain,
      "I have come to live as myself here in this wilderness,
      but in truth, I do not know how."

So a new apprenticeship began for him.
      First, they had told him, "You'd better lose that white tunic,"
      and then they went on to show him the seeds and berries,
      the roots and locust on which they foraged,
      and how to find honey by following bees to their hives,
      with which they sweetened it.
      They explained that the season on this high ground
      began with the rain in the spring, which strewed it with flowers
      and made it lush with grass, which was why
      they brought their sheep up here each year.
      The bounty would stretch into the summer moons,
      until dryness and a growing chill would bring it to an end
      and send them to seek pasture in the valley below.
      He studied with intensity to learn their ways,
      sought to harden himself to demands of their work,
      strove to vulgarize his speech with their aid,
      without which he could hardly hope to ask help,
      or, if ever he had something to say, to preach it.

Before long, upon reaching the bottom, they parted their ways,
      each seeking in the waning summer a place to settle in,
      the young man telling them as they parted,
      "Don't bother begging from the Essenes. It's not worth the trouble,"
      which filled this bittersweet parting with a roar of laughter.

Their way tended south toward Qumran;
      his veered north, toward the Jordan.
      As he crossed it, the luxury of flowing water
      passed through him, and he thought of the many mikvahs
      in the foundation of Qumran, which were suddenly reduced
      in his mind to pale imitations of what he had just experienced.
      He thought of this washing as a preparation
      for the distinctly new home on the other side,
      in wilderness, beyond Bethany.
      After a lengthy search, he had found a cave
      with a spring nearby and an abundance of seeds and berries,
      so he settled in to attend to the holy silence he had sought.

IV
The Master of the Wilderness

What the wilderness taught him was
      that the text ended in silence,
      that the ritual ended in silence,
      and that the priest ended in silence,
      which is not what he had been taught at Qumran.

      There the text was mined and collected
      into flowing florilegia, unbreakable chains,
      lists that turn back on themselves in order to preclude silence.
      But the text that leads not into silence
      cannot give rise to the question that must be asked.

      There the ritualized life was endlessly repeated
      and invariably explained, as what it had meant,
      and how it should make one feel, avoiding any silence
      in which a personal choice might be made
      that would change behavior into a free act.

      There priests, the despised ones in charge of the temple,
      were fiercely denounced,
      while the respected ones were nurtured in their sacred order
      and lavishly praised
      as the ones who would one day replace the former,
      thanks to *their* messiah, thus avoiding a silence
      that would give way to the people's response
      and that would bind the people to the priest as one.

      The great Essene enterprise, of which he had been so long a part,
      had come crashing down in the silence afforded by the wilderness,
      and in its place began to rise up a vision of *a* messiah
      who would come out of the silence and make all things new.

In the more recent days of his stay,
      he had begun having a recurring dream.
      It would begin with the sensation of flowing water,
      and in time it would resolve into the form of a river,
      on whose banks he would be standing filled with wonder,
      only to become aware that he was not alone

but in the company of the strangest gathering of people he had ever seen,
and they were expecting him to say or do something, what, he did not know,
except that it made him progressively uneasy, until he would awake
drenched in sweat but be relieved that it was just a dream
and that he could go on with his day.

Until, one day, he suddenly realized that the year in the wilderness
had turned and that spring was overtaking him.
It made him think of the boys in the scriptorium
and the masters at their table shut in or away
from the marvelous changes at work in the earth.
Did, he wondered, the Master of Cave still climb the cliff,
the only thing that troubled the interior waters on his return?

Then he thought, too, of his later mentors, the shepherds,
who would now be making preparations to move to the high ground,
and probably joking about the masters of Qumran,
whom they were about leave behind, and perhaps even of him,
that strange boy who wondered into their camp above the cliffs.
That brought him to a thought about himself and what he was doing.
It was suddenly clear that it was time for him to move like them.
Gathering the few things that he had, he took leave of his cave
and its spare but gracious setting that had provided living for the year,
and he made way to the river.

V
The Man at the River

His walk out of the wilderness had been filled
    with his remembrances of the river, that stream of living water
    that was mimicked by the mikvahs across the land,
    carefully contrived to pour a minimal flow from one side to the other
    and nowhere as ubiquitous or as utilized as at Qumran.
    When he arrived at the river, he waded into it,
    stooped, and cupped water in his hand and let it pour
    over his head to the sweet delight of his soul.
    He was, as it were, quite oblivious to the presence of others
    standing on the opposite bank, who took to staring at him.
    As if suddenly awakened, he saw them,
    a dozen or so loosely grouped at the far end of the ford:
    a pair of young men in the white tunics of the Qumran,
    at the other end a few whose accented speech betrayed them
    as peasants from the Galilee, and between them
    a motley assortment of humanity, people of the land!

Their stare made him suddenly aware of his appearance,
    a year's worth of hair and a tangled beard,
    a tunic fashioned from pelts and a girdle from leather.
    From somewhere inside of him welled up a rebuke:
    "What did you expect to see?
    Those who wear linen and fine clothes live in palaces."
    And continuing in the way of an explanation, he said,
    "I am a voice crying in the wilderness."
    The puzzlement on their faces led to insight:
    "You are seekers, I see, looking
    like all of land for the Messiah.

    "You in the tunics of the Essenes are looking for a priestly messiah,
    the restoration of the Zadok line of high priests,
    who will reform the temple according to your detailed study,
    and he will recruit you, the remnant of restored and washed
    priestlings, into his holy service.

    "You, with the accents of Galilee, are looking for a kingly messiah
    who will restore the throne of David, as you imagine it,
    and will enlist you, the true Israel, tested men of valor,
    to soldier in his holy army.

"You, people of the land, are looking for the gift-bearing messiah
who will give you the meat and drink for which you lust
and will call you lowly beggars to be the guests
at his holy banquet table."
Off to the side of the group, one robed in black,
a Pharisee, had called out mockingly,
"So, then, are you the Messiah?"
and had quickly stepped back into a shadow
to watch smiles spread across the faces of the group.
But they had hardly got underway before they collapsed
at the sound of the voice of the man, who firmly said,
"I am not."

And after silence, continued,
"You say you seek the Messiah,
but I say to you that you seek your own dream,
and when the 'one who is to come' comes,
who will be defined not by you or by me
but by himself,
you will not know him.
Only those who have prepared,
who have emptied themselves
and repented their sins—
only they will see him.

At that, the Pharisee had turned and walked off,
but two of the Galileans and one of Essenes walked up to him,
and when they reached him, they said,
"Please be our teacher?"
And, saying nothing in reply, he bent down
and brought up water with his hand
and poured it over their heads.

APHORISM §36 JESUS: STORY AND MYTH

A story becomes a myth when it stops being told and begins to be recited in an invariable form.

It is true that the Jesus story has been mythologized. This mythologizing began with accepting a vagueness in a response to some of the story's most powerful claims. This eased the difficulty of propagating the message in a culture that was tuned to mythology.

This accounts, to some degree, for the incredible and rapid gains of the Jesus moment, but it does not properly assess the profound and lasting losses for having done so.

The ultimate form of the mythologizing of the Jesus story is second-century Gnosticism, which finally resulted in a strenuous push back, imperfect and incomplete.

That is why demythologizing was a plausible agenda for someone like Rudolf Bultmann early on in the twentieth century.

Late in the twentieth century, the Jesus radicals, the so-called R group, were attempting to find a reality behind the ancient Jesus myth, as they were in a desperate flight from the punishment inflicted on them in their childhood by the prevailing Jesus myth.

I have even heard members of their party call for the remythologizing of the Jesus story, as if a modern myth was somehow better than an ancient myth! It is by bearing the burden of the story that anything of value for us can be found.

WATER TRANSFORMED
The New Skete, Cambridge, New York
January 6, 2020

———◆◆◆———

Our long journey home had hardly begun,
     when it paused for a day to observe the Theophany
     with those of the east who combine Christmas, Epiphany,
     and the Baptism of our Lord into one solemn feast.
     So high on a Taconic hill carved out by the Pumpkin Hook Kill
     and defined by the Howell McKie, on the edge of the Chestnut Woods,
     in the Temple of Holy Wisdom, with the brothers and sisters,
     we rose to listen to the celebrant sing at his entrance
     the song that declares that when Jesus was baptized,
     "the waters of the Jordan were transformed."
My heart was swept away by the poetry's unabashed sacramental reach,
     but my head, I confess, was caught by the thought, *How could this be?*
     Water must obey its nature, and hence it reacts as it must,
     indifferent to time and place set by any human doing or speech,
     or, for that matter, even one set by a god.
"But, head," I said, "you know nature is not so simple as that,"
     for from the beginning, when elements emerged
     and were bound, for example, as hydrogen and oxygen,
     there was written in them a code, a piece of a story, a part of the song,
     that in water and in everything else we call matter.
     When water spewed out of an ancient, fractured crust
          casting white feathers of vapor into the air,
          it shared with it a whisper: "I shall be seed."
     When water fell on the rock, pooled, and then out of a clef
          poured crystal rivulets across the floor,
          it declared with a roar, "I shall divide the earth."
     When water was enclosed in limpid chains, growing bodies,
          and fashioning faces, shining light round the world's girth,
          it uttered the song: "I shall give birth."
     Threads, lines, scales, call them as you will,
          unseen and half heard,
          rising and seeking to be part of a story
               until some day when they might be intersected
               by the trajectory of the man who would know them.

"Dear heart," my head replied, "I am well aware
        that science has undergone a transformation
        that has overcome the dualistic separation of mind and matter,
        but was not this science built on the former science of the ancients,
        so how would you have me believe that a man who came out of the Galilee
        and was baptized in the waters of an utterly unremarkable river
        would have anything to do with matter finding its voice and story?"
"O head, you still hesitate," heart chided. "You know very well
        that I know of the science of matter that existed long before that man lived.
        Indeed, all the ancients all had myths that contained degrees of science.
        The Greeks, it is true, took their form of the myth to new levels,
        which cumulated in Aristotle.
        So with this man you think to avoid this other man,
        but, head, you know perfectly well that it was Aristotle's science
        that had to be set aside to make way for the science of our day,
        breeched as was by balls falling from the Leaning Tower of Pisa!
        In the ancient science, matter was dead and unstoried.
        It was without a voice, or, if with a voice, one that was projected on it,
        as with a ventriloquist's trick, or with a mythic illusion
        where one hears one's own voice and calls it theirs.
But the science of living matter, whose story is being told,
        whose voice can be heard, is not so very old,
        certainly less old than the story about the man
        whose baptism we are celebrating in the sacred space.
        His story patterns the narrative, which was missing
        from the unseen and half-heard individuals of ancient world,
        as it was from all primal matter."
So, my heart dares to say it, it all began on this truly holy day,
        when a man's story was joined with theirs
        and matter was brought back from the dead
        and the true self was promised in the waters of life.

Subjecting Mary, Joseph, and John the Baptist to imagination, as we have in the earlier pieces of this section, may seem acceptable, where doing the same with Jesus is not. These, we are likely to admit, were embedded in their historical context not unlike we are in our own. But when it comes to Jesus, we are likely to hesitate to accept this. But a truly incarnate Christ must be embedded in a historical context, and what he knows about himself must be learned through experience. Otherwise, he is not like us in every way, save sin, as author of Hebrews has insisted.

Moreover, the following exercise in imagination deals with two heavily disputed questions: What was Jesus's relationship with John the Baptist? What was Jesus's understanding of himself as Son of God? Many have suggested that Jesus borrowed heavily from John the Baptist, while others, some as early as the New Testament itself, insisted that he gained nothing from John. In the same manner, the sonship question has caused a sharp division between those who contend that "Son of God" is late language appropriated from pagan mythology and those who claimed that Jesus knew in some a priori manner that he was God's Son. But it should be clear from an honest reading of the New Testament that Jesus did have a sense of sonship but that this sense is distinctly unlike the concept as it existed in pagan mythology. The task of imagination is to see if we can get a somewhat better handle on how John influenced Jesus and on what Jesus understood about his sonship.

I

In Search of John

Jesus had been asked on more than one occasion
    what he thought about John,
      that prophet who baptized people
    down along the Jordan.
    So it seemed necessary in time
      that he suspend his circuit in Galilee

and see for himself just who this John was.
It was not hard, of course, to find John.
He was the topic of conversation
from Herod's court to the nooks and crannies along the way.
As a result, Jesus was treated to a number of versions,
increasingly vivid, of this John
as he himself walked the crowded way
down the Jordan to where John was.

At last, he came to where John was preaching and baptizing,
not, he had to admit, without some hesitation,
for he had concluded long ago
that those who talked about messiahs
and of the coming of kingdoms
inevitably claimed to know, in no little detail,
the who and what the Messiah intended,
and consequently they were busy sorting out
those who would be in from those who would be out
and regimenting the world for his arrival.
This made it seem, Jesus thought with an inward smile,
unnecessary and even inconvenient
for their messiah to come.

Quietly he moved into the crowd of listeners who gathered around John.
What struck him first off was the mix that they were,
from all walks of life, halt, lame, tax collectors, prostitutes,
the poor and broken, the well and sleek,
officials from the courts of Herod,
earnest Pharisees from celebrated yeshivas,
who, of course, stood off at a distance by themselves.
John's words did not seem to devise and divide,
stern though they were.
They fell on all with equal weight,
which made the mix, at least for a moment,
realize that they were all in the same boat.
Of the Messiah John spoke in the most general way
as "the one who was to come,"
who it seemed was without lineage or agenda.
When the time came for those who had decided to be baptized
to come forward, they were all equally received,
apparently on the basis of what they were not.

So, after days of being a listener,
when the stir in the crowd began the procession,
he, too, arose and stood before John.

II
In the River

John looked down on the Hasid of Galilee,
of whose presence in the crowd
he had been well aware for some time.
The look of an itinerant healer from the country
was not all that difficult to recognize
for one educated among the elite priests of the city.
He was not a little puzzled as to why this Hasid had come to him.
His own mentors had taught him to hold such Hasids in contempt
as charlatans who believed in their own powers and little else,
who preyed on the weak and infirm,
whom they subsequently left in the lurch
with little more than an illusion of respite.
And he supposed the contempt would be returned
by the Hasids for such as the likes of him.
While he had broken with his mentors some time ago,
leaving behind their rigor for ritual and their zeal for messiahs,
he admitted to himself he retained not a little of their prejudices.

So he asked the Hasid bowed before him, "Why do you come to me?"
The Hasid replied, "Let it be so now, for it is proper for us
in this way to fulfill all righteousness."
By which he apparently meant
the rightness about relationships,
of he and him not separating
by means of a word
or by the act of baptizing,
or by not being baptized,
people, including themselves,
from one another.

Therefore, John laid his hand on the Hasid's shoulder
and pressed him down into the running waters of the river,
charging him to be prepared for the kingdom of God to come.

When the Hasid rose up out of the waters
and stepped up on that opposite shore,
it was if time had suddenly frozen.
In the length of an impossibly extended minute,
it had seemed to John that he had heard a silent roll of thunder.
It appeared from the stillness of the Hasid
that he, too, he had heard it
or something like it.
When the Hasid had stirred,
it was if he had awakened from an all-encompassing thought.
The Hasid looked off in the direction of wilderness,
where John himself had so recently lived,
as if he were attempting to find some landmark or path.
Having apparently found it, he had moved off in a most deliberate way,
set for the place where his glance had fallen.

III

In the Wilderness

The Hasid, newly washed, walked into the wilderness
wrestling with thoughts that raised questions
about whom he was and what he was called to do.
He was seeking the cave and the spring
where it was said John had stayed.
Guided by the talk in the crowd,
who had enumerated for him a number of landmarks,
he was confident that he had come to that very place
where John had lived on locust and wild honey.
It was there, he reasoned, that this child of a priestly family,
indoctrinated in the strict manner of the Essenes,
had transformed their messianic reasoning
into the simplicity of expecting a kingdom,
their exaggerated purity into a heartfelt repentance,
their rigorous and repeated ritual washing
into the casual flow of water once over the head.

He felt compelled to understand what in the wilderness
had worked this change in the child of a priest.
He hoped that it could do something similar
in the child of a carpenter

schooled, it was implied, in country living,
which would leave gaps in his knowledge,
informed with a rustic version of ritual,
a compromised practice of purity,
all alleviated by a rustic belief in messiahs.
Could the school of wilderness transform his heritage
into a coherent vision of a coming kingdom,
built from below by the healing
at which his hands were adept
and received from above in the grace
of an unexpected gift,
a birth, as it were, from above,
by the means of water and the spirit?
Spirit driven, he had soon found himself embedded in the wilderness.
It struck him first off
that it was more beautiful than anything he had ever seen
and yet that it could turn suddenly into something fearfully ugly—
how profound the pregnant silence was
and yet how suddenly it could yield to an anxious buzz.
In the buzz was the scratchy voice of the accusation
of the one called Satan, which rubbed the flesh
and clawed the mind,
leaving an itch
for pleasure, for power, or for glory.
Clearly it was in the beauty of this silence
that John had been transformed.
Somehow he had found a way to set aside the buzz.
It would be in the beauty of this silence
that he could find the fullness of the vision that he sought.
So he determined to banish the buzz
when it came with the power of the word.

In the span of some forty days,
it had wrought in him the union
between his compassion for healing
and his new passion for a kingdom come from above,
at last a single united message of love.
Once the message was secure,
the question followed:
To whom was it to be delivered,
and by whom was it to be spoken?

To Jerusalem?
By him?
Why him?
How them?
Surely they would ask him, "Who are you?"
And if he said, "Jesus of Nazareth," they would laugh,
"Can anything good come out of Nazareth?"
To this doubt, the silence replied with a smile.
If he said, "A prophet," they would rebut with scorn,
"Was it ever heard that a prophet would come from Galilee?"
The silence smiled again as if to say for sure.
If he said, "The Messiah," they would demand
proof of his lineage and a demonstration of his marching orders
that promised victory.
Once again, silence smiled in concurrence.
"Who, then?" he had asked in exasperation.
Silence replied, "Say you are the Son."
"Whose Son?" he asked.
"The Son of God or the Son of Man?"
Silence smiled and gently asked him, "Is there a difference?

IV
Out of the Wilderness

He walked out of the wilderness
with a clarity about who he was
and what he was called to do.
He crossed the Jordan
under the gaze of the baptist
and thought he heard John say to the two standing there,
"God's Lamb."
Like a new Israel,
he passed the ruins of Jericho
and took the serpentine ascent to Jerusalem.
At the center of his mind was the idea "I am the Son,"
across which his thoughts wandered
like the twists of the road
that sought to avoid a precipice.
On one side, it pulled back from Son of God,
and on the other side, from the Son of Man,

only to return to the common center:
"I am the Son."
But of whom?
Or could it be of both?

He arrived at the halfway point in the ascent,
at a place well known
to anyone who has ever taken this road,
where a spring pours crystal water from a rock,
and there he stepped off the road,
took a long draft of the chilled water,
and sat down for a rest.
In the relief from the climb,
his mind began to conceive a story.
The story started with a rich man or a king
who had gone to a far-off land or distant country,
leaving behind a vineyard,
one that he had planted and equipped with special care.
The man put it in the hands of tenants who would return his rent.
At first, they had done so, but in time, they had begun to short it,
and then not pay it at all.
The king—call him a king—
sent his servant to reason with them.
But they beat the king's servant and sent him home without a cent.
So after another try, the king said to himself, "I will send my son,
for surely they will respect my son."
Then it was time to go,
so he arose, to finish the story on another day,
and returned his feet to the serpentine road
and his head to its labored thoughts,
save for one last thought, which seem wholly certain
the story he had begun to compose that day
was already happening.

JOHN AT AENON

Now a discussion about purification arose between John's disciples and the Jews.
—John 3:25

⸺⬥⸺

With the warming of spring,
  John moved north
  from the lower reach of the Jordan,
  where he had wintered
  and had encountered that Hasid of Galilee
  who weighed very much on his mind.
  There at a spring named Aenon,
  a stream of water flowed, cool and abundant,
  falling out of the palisades,
  down onto the rock below,
  and over time it had carved a cauldron
  perfect for the purposes of baptizing.

What prompted the dispute is not clear.
  Perhaps John had been overheard
  comparing this living water
  to the captive waters of their mikvahs,
  which were constructed to mimic that flow
  by means of an upper and a lower pool,
  causing the water to stir, as if it were living.

Likely they had charged that such a casual washing,
  in a place so unprotected from passing pollutants,
  could hardly last more than moments
  before it would need to be redone.
But that, John thought, was precisely the point.
  Their endless ritual rewashings,
  fending off the onslaught of an ever-renewing
  assault of imagined pollutants, seemingly promising

that they might find themselves pure at the moment of judgment,
where what was needed was a single simple reversal
of course, bound for the judgment to come.
The Hasid of Galilee whom he had baptized
and who was now at work in Jerusalem and Judea
would understand that, he thought.

APHORISM §37 THE LOSS OF MYTH

What is lost when myth is purged from our attempts at grasping reality is the association of the spirit with nature. The disassociation of spirit and nature leaves a gnawing but poorly defined hunger in the spirit.

Thus, it appears that myth was a stage of human development that was not without its value.

If the text becomes a story, can the association of spirit and nature be saved? Suppose in the story the principal character reaches out with his hands and takes bread?

If one becomes incarnate, one accepts the risk of being crucified. Moreover, one accepts the risk of falling into the hands of historians, which makes one subject to endless revisions, dilations, and diminishments.

O SON

O Son of Man,
    the spitting image, as they say, of your father's face.
    O Second Adam, the originating energy of a whole new race,
    at last, with you the wall has been broken down.
O Son of God,
    the spitting image, as they say, of your father's face.
    O the very face of God, the originating energy of all,
    at last, with you all shall be in all.

HIGH ON A HILL

High on a hill above a lake called Kinnereth,
    high enough to see that water lies harp shaped,
    Jesus stands in the posture of a watcher.
What is it, my Lord, that you see?
    And a cry wells up in his frame,
    wrenching it as if to turn it inside out.
I see my friends below struggling at their oars,
    against a turbulent sea.
    I see a crowd hungering to be fed by me
    on these barren hills.
    I see veiled women looking to be free
    in a world of possibilities.
Oh, my God,
    what am I doing to these people?

TABOR

—————◆—————

Stepping away from his friends
       into an interior stillness, a silence
       and a darkness that he had long known,
       he found it filled
            with movement that went nowhere,
            with speech that said nothing,
            with light that casts no shadow
            and that inhabits no space.
Yet it was in this very moment that he knew that he was sent
       to preside over an exodus,
               to anoint successors,
                    and to make his departure.
Coming out of it, he saw his three friends
       looking at him with faces full of confusion and fear.
       One of them was struggling to say something to him.
       What was it that they saw? he wondered.

ONE WINTER

Prologue

Jesus therefore no longer walked openly among the Jews,
but went from there to a town called Ephraim in the region near the wildness.
—John 11:54

One winter in the orchards of Ephraim,
      a place deserted save for a few rustics,
      yet no more than a day's walk from the city
      in which he had been hunted and stoned,
      the Word of God came for a stay,
      a solitary retreat, save for the Twelve,
      lasting as many days as it would take
      for the will of his Father to become known,
      in a hidden space, for a needed time, to pray.

Why It Must Be a Crucifixion

It was in this winter retreat
      in the orchards of Ephraim
      when it had become perfectly clear
      why he had not died in the temple
      under the weight of stones
      hurled by an incensed mob.

      That would have been a death,
      sudden and largely unseen,
      a fleeting moment
      in whose aftermath,
      the state and the cult
      would have issued denials,
      brushing the matter aside
      as an unfortunate thing no one's fault.

But a crucifixion, say, at the coming feast,
>would be an altogether different matter.
>He had, of course, seen crucified men.
>Who in Israel had not?
>It had, after all, not been owned by the Romans
>for the exceptional cases of messiahs,
>misfits, or rebels with and against their order.
>They crucified murders and thieves
>and others they just didn't like.
>They did it in a way so it would be seen,
>which is why they preferred
>an ugly little hill called Calvary,
>outside of Jerusalem's front door.
>It was their intent that those who looked on the crucified
>experience the grim exchange of having their looks returned.

Yes, he had seen it,
>often, perhaps,
>but with this difference: most
>who had looked on such bodies
>contorted on a cross
>saw them as already corpses,
>albeit living ones.
>But he, in his habit of empathy,
>would have seen the man!
>Would have even entered into the man
>in such a way as to have already been on a cross,
>whose wood, he would have learned, could be sweet,
>even if its geometry, he did not doubt,
>could be most cruel.

That is what made a crucifixion at the coming Passover
>a confrontation that could change the world.
>It would not be deniable by the cult or the state

or quickly and neatly whisked from the stage.
It would begin a revolution.

It was, of course, not impossible for the state or the cult
to come to that line and turn back,
making for a soft revolution
by the means of renouncing death in their art.

It was even worth a prayer:
"Remove this cup from me."
But definitely not to be counted on.

Thus were his thoughts
on that first day of the winter retreat
in the orchards of Ephraim.

The Moon Was Full

Long into the night, they had talked
about things done and things to come.
Then, before their lying down,
he had sought the night air
to restore an interior silence.
And glad he was for doing so,
for he had stumbled on a sight
of dark laced limbs in the orchard
washed with silver light.

The moon was full.
The next full moon, he thought, would be
the last time for him to see this silver spread,
for that light would be from Passover's moon,
and he would be not in a woods but in the city
and without the time to become part of the light
with which its streets and wall would be dressed.

He would be hanging on a tree,
becoming part of the dark
that must come before the light
that would make humans free.

The Last Passover

The thought of a coming Passover
caused him to remember
the question that must be asked,
that he had often been asked as a child.
His answers had been coached by the man
who had fathered him
and rewarded by the smile of the woman
who had mothered him.

"Why is this night different from all other nights?"
      Why the lamb is slain?
      Why the bread in haste is made?
      Why the cup four times is poured?
The answers to which he had quickly mastered
and even now he could recite with fearful virtuosity.

But on this coming Passover, if they were answered by rote,
they would strike a hollow note
and break his heart by their inadequacy,
for this coming night would be different
from all other nights
because it would bring his dying day.

But then maybe these answers had never been
quite enough after that first night in Egypt,
for they had always left unspoken the ways
that the days that followed would
or should be different from all other days.

And if they weren't, wouldn't it explain
how ephemeral their being as a people had become
and how fleeting their freedom had been,
shaken, as it were, the very next night
while they stood at the edge of the sea,
and then desiccated, as it were, in the years
spent wandering in a wilderness?

It had, of course, been death and the fear of death.

That shook their sense of peoplehood, that night at the Red Sea,
when they feared that they would be slain by Pharaoh's army.
Fiercely they had wished that Moses had left them alone,
and they longed to be back in Egypt's servitude.

That sucked the life out of their freedom in the wilderness,
where they feared the gnawing hunger and the thirst.
Narcissistically they nursed a longing
to return to Egypt's very flesh pots.

That returned them year after year to the unchanged day
that followed the night that they had called different
and to the trading in the death of others in place of their own,
until their very own land shared in Egypt's lot.

What then would be different about this coming Passover night—
  if he sat with the Twelve in Jerusalem,
  what could he say?
Say, he thought,
  I the lamb will be.
  I the bread will break.
  I the cup will fill.

Would they then remember
    that he had become the lamb,
    that he could be recognized when they broke the bread,
    that his life had been poured into the cup from which they drank?
When they walked away
    from this coming Passover meal, singing Hallel,
    they would come, as did they of old, to their own Red Sea,
    where they themselves would face a sudden death.
    He would die it for them so they could cross on.

And after they had crossed that sea,
    and he had left them for the last time,
    a wilderness would stand astride their paths
    where they would be diminished by the wear of time.
    He would send them a comforter so they would remember.

That is, he thought,
    why that night would be different from all other nights,
    why he would be the Last Passover,
    and why the day that followed would be at last the Day,
    different as it were from all other days.

The Watcher Bloomed

He had spent the day with one of the Twelve
in the orchard, following the pruners, whose hooks
expertly brought down the superfluous branches
of its trees so that their fruit might be full and in reach,
as they did with dispatch every day of the dormant season.

He with his companion had gathered the fallen limbs
and stacked them neatly in the far corner of the field,
where they could be retrieved at a later, less demanding time
for use in the homes of the caretakers, and, with their leave,
to take to the widow on whose farm they were staying,
a small but welcome help to both.

And for him and his companion, the stooping and bending had felt good.
It had dispelled the chill and the drag of a winter day,
substituting for a while a physical endeavor for the mental one
that stood for him at the heart of this retreat,
until the pruners for the lack of light had gone early to their rest.

He and his companion had each bound a great bundle of wood
and, putting them on their backs, made their way to the widow's cottage.
Upon crossing the hedge that separated the orchard from the road,
they saw the "watcher" among the bare wood, covered in blushed pinks.

A smile came across his face, and he asked his companion,
"What do you see?"
"I see the branch of an almond tree,"
his companion, in on the game, replied with glee.
"Well, you have seen."
And then he had said,
"My Father has just spoken."
"What?" inquired the companion,
surprised at the turn the conversation had taken.
"He has just said to us, has he not,
'I am watching over my word to perform it'?" (Jeremiah 1:11).

Why I Will Not Speak

As he continued to walk from the field
      to the widow's cottage and then to the cave,
      which served as their shelter for the length of their stay,
      where they would indeed lay down the burden of the day,
      he mused to himself.
The Watcher had indeed seen it,
      what no one else had yet seen,
      the movement in the dead wood.
      He had seen it and announced it:
      "A tree of bare wood would bloom!"
It would be done, as God had willed it,
      and yet there would be a trial,
      or trials, or the pretense of trials.
      Should he not now somehow
      be preparing his defense?
But the real trial had already happened,
      and the trials to come would be about
      how a certain cable of priests and their learned advisers
         would regard themselves in the aftermath
            and would be regarded by those who followed them.
      About how a certain governor and his court
         would feel about themselves
         and what their peers would come to say
         about what they had done that day.

If with his words he could confuse or divide the court,
      could cajole or convince his judges to act against their will,
      it would yield a temporary victory, doing nothing
      except confirming the way of the world
      and making no change, and no kingdom would come.

In the end, it was they who needed his words.
      They would use his words to justify themselves.
      Whatever words he spoke to them in his defense,
      they would twist and spin into an admission of guilt.
      And whatever words he spoke against them,
      they would spin and twist into self-evident treason.

The only thing that they could not twist or spin
would be his silence. Only his silence
would force them to own what they were doing,
and only his silence could raise among them a sense of guilt
that might lead them, or perhaps one of them, to dissent,
even if for a moment, which would be in itself a victory,
a beneficent gift to the kingdom to come.

Clearly this was a frail hope,
but as important to hold as any hope in the world.
"I will not speak," he resolved.

The result of his reasoning made him think of a psalm,
one that they had sung together the other night.
It had struck him at the time, he remembered,
that the memoirist, who was leading them,
was showing off a bit by taking them
to such an unfamiliar psalm.

The words began "I said I will keep watch
upon my ways, so that I do not offend with my tongue."
And then the psalm came to the line
"I will put a muzzle on my mouth while the wicked man is before me."

It was those particular words—
"I will put a muzzle on my mouth
while the wicked man is before me"—
that had caught his attention.
Since then, these words
had been tumbling around in his head,
and he had been wondering why.
But now they had come home to support
his resolve that whatever the trial,
he would not speak.

Red Anemones

Red anemones unseen had run
    across the orchard floor.
    Hermon's dew had raised in the night,
    and they had been opened by the morning sun.
    Unseen he had sought the ridge before the light
    in search of some solitary time to pray.
    Then, having turned to face the day,
    he had come upon this unexpected sight.
Stopping to take in the reddened floor,
    he thought, *How graced this winter wood!*
    As graced the world would be, he hoped,
    when from the rood his blood would pour.

How Death Will Speak

All the night before, he had heard in his head
    the words that the troubled psalmist had once said:
    "What gain is my blood,
        my going down to corruption?"
    The psalmist's words had continued to trouble the solitude
    that he had sought in the morning air.
    What terrible doubt is this!
        Was this a question the psalmist had put to God
        to weigh the absence of his praise?
        Or was this a question put for these later days,
        to expose his own doubts that God could raise
            him from his descent on the day of favor
            God had promised in his word?

This, at least, he thought was clear.
    The fear of silence compels some persons
    to be so excessively verbal just before their deaths,
    rushing to their own defense
    and not trusting the silence.

    Yet the hope in silence allows other persons
    to be so exquisitely still before their deaths,
    waiting for their defense to come
    and trusting God that it would.

Had not the psalmist also said,
    "Lord, you raised my soul from Sheol;
    you caused me to live after my descent into the pit"?
    This was, he thought, the very hope he had recently drawn
    from that burst of red that had greeted that morning's dawn.

    Now, having returned to where they assembled for the morning prayer,
    they together had begun the praise with the appointed words

        "My God, the soul which you gave me is pure," which ends
            with "the Lord, the one who restores souls to dead corpses."

They stood for some time in silence,
    as if to weigh those words,
    and then he asked them if they could next say
    the psalm that begins "My God, my God."

    And the one among them whose memory was like a book
    coached them until the psalm began to flow.
    "My God, my God, why have you forsaken me?"

When they had come to its end,
    he asked them, "Do you think the psalmist
    intended to describe a death on a cross?"
    Opinion was divided, but in the end, they had agreed
    that whatever death the psalmist had imagined,
    it was certainly like the death one
    would have died from being crucified.
"Then tell me: What do you think," he asked them
    of the one whom the psalmist described,
    "had he lived, or had he died?"
    Surely he had lived! they promptly replied,
    for the psalmist asserted that God had answered his prayer
    and that the man himself recounted to his brothers
    in the midst of the great congregation
    the power of God's name.
Still, he rejoined, the psalmist said of him
    that he was set in the dust of death,
    that his tongue cleaved to his mouth,
    and that his bones were wrenched apart.
    "I wonder, then, in what body he did speak—
    to what congregation?

And why it was that in the end the congregation
was described as seed
and as the generation yet to come
and as a people yet unborn.
Indeed, it seems that death did speak
to the dead and to the yet unborn."

They stood in silence for a good while struggling to follow his drift.
While in his mind the conviction formed: "The hour is coming
when all who are in their grave will hear his voice and will come out" (John 5:29).
After which he said matter-of-factly,
"Tomorrow, we will leave the orchards of Ephraim."

Epilogue

As you know, they were seen
on the high road that leads to Jerusalem.
And it was reported that "he was walking ahead of them"
and that they seem to be amazed
but at the same time "were afraid" (Mark 10:32).
Indeed, the Word of God would be broken,
and the silence of God would return.
Till it would thunder.
Three times it would thunder.
After which the Word of God would look up
and read on God's face these words:
"Arise, my love, and come,
for now the winter is past."

IMMANUEL

Deep in the interior of the most ancient
　　and profoundly silent being of God
　　was the Word whose intent
　　was to become flesh
　　before flesh was
　　and in so doing
　　to die in that flesh
　　so that flesh could be in God.

APHORISM §38 NARRATIVE AND DOCTRINE

An era of church history began when a certain form of doctrine began to drive narrative out of the center of what constitutes church.

The best defense for doctrine is that it defends the narrative. An example of this is the development of the creeds, but once past creeds, doctrine begins to become problematic.

The recovery of the narrative's role at the center of church life has taken place in a series of fits and starts. Two of the most interesting examples in the Western church are the life of St. Francis of Assisi and the early reforms of Martin Luther. Yet how quickly the addiction to doctrine stifled such recoveries, among both the Franciscans and the Lutherans.

In what does the addictive power of doctrine lie? The rush of certainty!

TELLING BEADS

Of the humble beadsman,
 who earns his bread
 by saying rosaries for the dead,
it was said,
 "He tells his beads."
Even in this pious craft of old,
 it was not lost that what saves
 is the story being told.

THE CONVERSION OF PAUL

Part 1
He Stood on the Edge of the Field

> Then they dragged him out of the city and began to stone him, and the
> witnesses laid their coats at the feet of a young man named Saul.
> —Acts 7:59

He stood on the edge of the field,
      a hand on his chin testing, or hiding,
      the fuzz that had not yet become a beard,
      a thing he could not understand, given the fact
      that his mind thought like a man
      well beyond his years.
He had followed the men, his teachers and friends,
      out of the synagogue where the man had been condemned,
      certain that he himself would be among those to cast stones.
      But the men had stopped him, saying he was too young.
      As consolation, they appointed him guardian of their coats.
Left looking at the man who had been made to kneel in the field,
      he could not believe his ears that he still blasphemed,
      calling on that man Jesus to forgive them their sin,
      calling him Lord as if he were no less than God's son.
      What else could they have done except silence him with stones?
He had not, however, reckoned with the sight of a dying man,
      the fact being so inexplicably more complex than he had imagined.
      It shook him to the core, so he called on rage

to blind his eyes from seeing the man on the ground
and to ring in his ears to mask the sound
of a dying man's prayer.
Then and there he swore that he would prove by word and deed,
beyond any doubt, the utter necessity of this act
that he was witnessing that day.
He would lift from their error those victims
who had been led into the false way,
the one attributed to that Jesus,
who was, it was clear, no son.

Part 2
He Rode on a Horse

Now as he was going along and approaching Damascus, suddenly a
light from heaven flashed around him. He fell to the ground and heard
a voice saying to him, "Saul, Saul, why do you persecute me?
—Acts 9:3

He rode on a horse,
the unmistakable sign of his mission's import,
on the road to Damascus to where he was sent.
Back ridged, mind fixed, rehearsing as he went
the counterarguments so carefully honed
as to cut to the very bone
where heretical faith was joined,
severing the blatantly specious argument
that someone had been shown
to be God's son.
Then, unexpectedly,
the rigidity of his back
and the fixity of his mind broke
and he was laid on the ground,
eyes unseeing and mind unthinking.
In his mind remained juxtaposed

the two towering arguments,
the sound of a strange voice
and a recollection of a great light,
but not the impetus to move
them on, apart or together.
His party had taken him and laid him in a bed,
where he lay troubled by his not seeing,
but more undone by his not thinking.
He had lain there until a strange man,
fearful and shy, had come,
saying that he had been sent.
After the man had prayed,
light had come into his eyes
and through them into his mind.
In that very moment, he saw
what he had not seen in a very long time:
a primal thought
so utterly pure and pristine
that it was a perfect mirror
reflecting the one who had called it to be,
to be an image of God,
to be a firstborn,
a son,
a Word,
God.
Oh, my God, he is the Son!

Part 3
He Stepped out of the Basket

The governor under King Aretas guarded the city of Damascus in order to seize me, but
I was let down in a basket through a window in the wall and escaped from his hands.
—2 Corinthians 11:32

After some time had passed, the Jews plotted to kill him, but their plot became known to Saul.
They were watching the gates day and night so that they might kill him; but his disciples took
him by night and let him down through an opening in the wall, lowering him in a basket.
—Acts 9:23

He stepped from the basket
      onto the road heading south,
      watching in the dim night light for the fork
      that would take him on the less-traveled way
      into Arabia.
As he went, he replayed in his mind
      the deliberations that had brought him to this point.
      He could not stay in Damascus
      for daily his presence added to the anxiety and fear
      of that small community that had taken him in.
      Anxiety had arisen
      because it was hard to see how he could fit,
      and fear because of the growing threat
      of the authorities, who were demanding
      that they turn him over to them or suffer for it.
He could not return to Jerusalem
      for there his presence would
      surely enrage the high priests
          whose mission he had undertaken and aborted;
      embarrass his Pharisaic brothers
         with whom he had studied;
      and trouble that larger, original community of saints,
         which he had persecuted.
He could not go home to Tarsus
        for there he would face his family,
        pained by the way he had shattered the dream of his father.
That is why the fork in the road was the only way
      to avoid the Nabatean king who sought him,
      or going to the homes to which he was not ready to return.
On finding the fork, he went to the left,
      setting himself for Arabia,

and yet turning his mind
to those he was leaving behind.
That strange and lovely little man name Ananias,
who, having the courage of a holy fool,
had come to and dared enter the house called Judah,
the house of the Pharisaic school, in which he lay.
The man's prayer had given him his sight.
Then he had given him his hand,
and he had led him out into the open air,
down the street, to a much humbler house,
where new friends took him in.
Strange, too, were they, he mused,
for not many had been wise or rich
or among the powerful of that city—
some had in fact been taken in off the street
where they had begged or prostituted themselves.
A motley crew, stones gathered from an open field.
So unlike him and his student friends, square-cut
quarried rock from the finest stone,
and each of them so like the other.
The only way one had to be different
was by the degree of zeal,
which was precisely what the quarriers had wished
Oh, how he had excelled in that!
His masters were bent on building a wall,
a great wall to shut in and shut out.
But this other motley crew sought
nothing more than to be laid by some hidden hand
into the shape of a free and movable altar
like the one once laid in the ancient Israel.
How, then, could he ever hope to fit in with these?
Unless he lay for some spell in an open field,
subject to the heat and the cold,
to the wind and the rain,
until he be better worn and rounded,

losing his edges and corners
and better able to trust in an unseen hand
to fit his irregularity with those of others
so as to form the quintessential altar.
"O Arabia, the land of the hapless Hagar, the mother of bondage,
you," he had prayed, "are my hope. You are the field
in which time and elements will work on me,
doing what I cannot do for myself,
the weathering and breaking
and the ultimate making
of a new man in me."

Part 4
Paul in Arabia

God was pleased to reveal his Son to me, so that I did not confer with any human being, nor
did I go up to Jerusalem to those who were apostles before me. But I went at once into Arabia.
—Galatians 1:14

A veil of thick darkness hangs over St. Paul's visit to Arabia.
—Lightfoot, "Commentary on St. Paul's Epistle to the Galatians," p. 127

He sat in the back room of the Arab's house.
He had spotted that man
in the bazaar of that first small desert town
to which he had come.
Noticing that the man's hands bore
the telltale marks of a maker of tents,
he had made bold and asked him for work.
"Why should I need your work?" the Arab had shot back.

In reply, Paul had pulled the tools of his trade from under his cloak
and said, "Because I am good
and because I should rather work than beg."
Now in the course of an afternoon
that had neither a number nor a name,

his hand was methodically pulling at the needle
leading a coarse thread through the irregular hides
that needed to be fitted and secured to each other
in order to form a square that could cover a frame
set in the field by some Bedouin, soldier, or sojourner.

He found himself observing the rise and fall of his own hand
and thinking of his father, whom he had left behind
when he had gone to yeshiva in Jerusalem.
"Ah, such a privilege!" his father had said to him.
"They will fill your head with the Torah in letters,
but do not forget that your hands have
their own way of knowing the Torah in things,
for everything that is made
is laced and held together by Torah.
The true craftsman learns to love Torah in things."
Then, in a particular point in the cycle,
the hand at its apogee stopped,
or seemed to have stopped.
The external sight was paired
with an internal flash of light,
like the light at his fall onto the road,
which he now knew more accurately
was the flash of a face.
For a brief moment, he was
again caught by the regard
of Christ for the world.
In the aftermath of this brief insight, he thought,
If the Torah in things comes from the face,
would not the Torah in script come to the same place?
Torah wherever it is found must lead to the face,
and the face to Torah.
To gain Christ
is not to lose Torah.
Of this he was now utterly sure.

Part 5
He Rose to Return

And afterwards I returned to Damascus.
—Galatians 1:17
Then after three years, I did go up to Jerusalem to visit Cephas and stayed with him fifteen days.
—Galatians 1:18
Then I went into the region of Syria and Cilicia.
—Galatians 1:21
When the believers learned of it, they brought him down to Caesarea and sent him off to Tarsus.
—Acts 9:30

He rose from the bench in the Arab's back room
and emphatically declared to himself then and there,
"I shall go home."

"No longer am I hewn stone,
but fieldstone weathered and worn,
rejected by the master builders
who have the illusion that they would build a new world.

"I am ready for grace, as it were, or at least
I am reduced, God knows, to no hope but grace.

"No longer am I the voice of a faceless gospel
of moving stories and lofty words learned by rote,
of the wisdom of the wise, or of the rulers of this present age,
which is without the light that laces words and syntax
to their origin, God knows, to no thing but face.

"No longer am I the keeper of an ancient Torah,
veiled from the face that had uttered it,
whose very words I once took as warrant to do violence to others
but now find as Torah written in all hearts,
making us under the law and those apart from the law
nothing less than brothers."

He had spied out the words of the way that they called gospel

in order to shred them, to the terror of those on that way
and to the delight of his masters and school friends.
After his conversion, he had sought to impress
his new friends in Damascus
with what he knew of their way.
What he once mocked he could now commend
with great power.
Happily, he had felt his old zeal rise up within him,
until he noticed his new friends winching.
He had realized at once that violence could be done
with these new words as well,
God forbid!
He could see that his new self could become nothing more
than his old self, only seven times worse.

But at last the air and the dark of Arabia
had caused him to see the light,
the light deep in his mind,
leading back through the words,
whether of Torah or gospel, or both,
to a face, the holy face of God.

Which is itself the Gospel,
the one that is neither taught nor received from men,
and because of that, he could be really new
and ready to live by grace
and, God help him, to do no violence.

So which, Paul asked himself,
was the home that he was ready to face?
Distant Tarsus, where he had been born;
divided Jerusalem, where he had been schooled;
or nearby Damascus, where he had been reborn?

First, he would return, he thought, to Damascus,

the latest and most gracious of these homes.
There it would soon show in the faces of his new friends,
or not, if he was ready to live by grace.
Then, he continued, the time would come to go to Jerusalem,
that transient home where he had studied Torah
and been led by disordered zeal to persecute the Way.
There it would show in the faces of those to whom he had been an enemy
if his Gospel was in vain or not.
Finally, he would return, he supposed, to the city
nestled between the sea and the mountains
where he had been born and schooled on his father's knee.
There he would know in the faces of family and old acquaintances
if his Gospel had the power to call new friends out of old.

THE SONG OF THE THREE MATTHEWS

———◆◆◆———

I should like to sing you the song of three Matthews,
     of the apostle, of the prophet, and of the scribe,
     divided by age, distinct in function, and separated by time
     and yet allegedly held to be one.
First, I would sing of the man who sat in the booth
     collecting the imperial tax along the shore of the Galilee,
     the owner of a great house where he hosted the Nazarene
     famous for declaring the kingdom of heaven opened to all—
     of the man who walked out of the booth and away from the house
     to follow that Nazarene to the foot of the cross
     and then to be sent to the lost sheep of Israel and more,
     only to end in the schooling of a generation of new prophets
     learned in the testimonies of the ancient prophets
     and rehearsed in the sayings of the Nazarene.
Second, I would sing of the man called prophet
     who wandered the Galilee visiting the households
     that had taken the Nazarene in as their Lord,
     comforting them with the explication of the prophesies
     made in the former times by the prophets of Israel,
     and confirming them with the sayings
     made in recent times by Lord of the kingdom of heaven.
     He presided over their sacred meals
     and ordered the heads of their homes
     where they waited for the kingdom to come on earth.
     In time, he had marshaled an army of visiting prophets,
     sending them out not only in the Galilee
     but far north into the land of the Syrians.
Third, I would sing of the man who kept school
     in the heart of the Galilee,
     shaping a text partly received and partly expanded
     with the testimonies in which he had been schooled
     and with the oral sayings that he had committed to memory

so that the overseers and elders of the merging household
    could keep church no longer dependent on itinerant prophets,
    of which he himself once was, or, better, the student of one,
        who were now declining in number and worth.

The apostle saw the passing of his age
    and was replaced by the itinerant prophets,
    some of whom he had schooled
    and others whose learning he doubted.
The prophet saw the end of his days
    and was replace by elders and overseers,
    some of whom he had ordered
    and others whose ordering he feared.
The scribe saw the end of his task
    and was consequently replaced by his text,
    which he had placed in the hand of elders and overseers,
    with which they could normalize and defend their lives,
    but also, he saw, could turn it against life itself.
Who, then, could imagine that these three could be a single author,
    separate by method and by time, as they were?
    Moderns are quick to insist that their doubt is based on the reason
        that it is impossible for them to imagine such individuals,
        unique in person and separated by years, to be a single author.
    But it appears to me that the ability to imagine a Matthew
        is somehow connected to their insistence that they themselves
        cannot be known by anyone else,
        even as they pretend not to know anyone else.
        Out of such modern solecism, no imagination can come,
        as in the ancient hell, no imagination could be born.
    Still, I must say that I have imagined it,
        even as I am poorly known and poorly know
        and as I wait for the light in which I will be known
        and will fully know—
        imagined, that is, that the three are indeed a single author!

The Final John

I, John, known for writing bad Greek laced with Hebrew syntax
    and speaking poor Greek accented with Aramaic inflections,
    I am your brother who shares with you the persecution of the Roman age,
    which may seem new to you, but, to me, all that I have ever known.

I, you will recall, was a resident of Jerusalem who lived through the siege
    that the Romans set against it, five months of abject terror and famine,
    ending only late in August, when they breached the northwest wall
    and poured slaughter and destruction down that city's streets.

My community, the mother Church of John, had decided to stay
    when others chose to flee, for we loved that city,
    its paving on which our Lord had walked,
    the temple's porch in which he had talked,
    and the gardens in which he had knelt to pray.

We were not rebels, who were divided and fought each other,
    who demanded the greater share of supplies, and who had even
    willfully destroyed them, thinking to put pressure on us to fight.
    We kept our peace and chose instead the role of witness.

When the breach had come, our elders summoned me,
    yet a lad, an apprentice scribe, and they charged me
    to carry the apocalypse that they were writing at that time to you
    so that the world could know of our peril and could brace for their own.

With the scroll bound to my chest, they slipped me
    out the dung gate in the lower southwest wall,
    counting on the rout in the north to have lowered the vigilance
    that Romans had kept these many months, ensuring any escapee
    would end up crucified before the walls for us to see.

That is when I came to you, the elder daughter of the Church of John,
    here on Asia's rich shores, where the apostle himself had died.
    You took me in and hung on my words about Jerusalem's fate
    and about the evil an imperial Rome posed to free people everywhere.

True to my elders' commission to bring you their witness,
      I tried to tell you that what Jerusalem suffered would come
      in time to you as well, but I saw in time how you came to regard
      Jerusalem to be an odd and distant fact with little to do with you.

When you asked, "When?" I would say, "Soon."
      Soon not as quantifiable time but as an overshadowing reality.
      And now it has come. Antipas is dead. Our churches are under siege.
      I am in Patmos, and more exiles and more deaths will follow.

Therefore, receive from me this apocalypse that I have sent you.
      It was begun by my elders in Jerusalem and entrusted to me.
      It has become my life's work and will be complete on the last Lord's Day.

It calls you to stand firms as witnesses.
      How, you will ask, is that enough? I say, "It is the all."
      Those who counsel reason will be complicit with it,
      and those who counsel resistance will be used by it.
      The one thing that the imperial order cannot bare is witnesses.

When, you will ask, will it end? I say, "Soon."
      After the last unsealing, after the final trumpet,
      after the pouring of the seventh bowl, then the imperial order
      will itself fall and our city, the new Jerusalem, will rise.

O JUDAICA

O Judaica, had you not survived,
> I would not know the mother of my savior.
> They dressed her in brocade renaissance robes
> and pronounced her the queen of heaven
> when all along she was an earthly handmaiden
> dressed in worsted wool, plain clothes.

> Is it because of this that they have resented you
> and thought the world, their world, better without you?
> Smugly they quote your rabbi,
> the great Gamaliel, in their favor,
> but fail to see that turned around,
> it pronounces your survival
> to be the work of God as well.

O Judaica, you I would celebrate with a solemn feast.

APHORISM §39 ANTISEMITISM AND SEMITICISM

The persistence of antisemitism is both depressing and inexplicable. One would have thought that the Nazi Holocaust, whose inhumanity was so grotesque and whose futility so self-evident, would ensure that antisemitism could never again find any following. But that is clearly not the case, as it continues to resurface precisely in those places that should know better. It has such a hold as to cause one to wonder whether it has not become an inherent element of Western society. God forbid. How can they not see that this is a self-defeating, crass politics that uses people's misfortune to their own ends? Parallel to antisemitism is Semiticism. The latter is as old as the fifth century BCE and the laws of Ezra. We all need to get over this.

AN UNCOMFORTABLE ORDER

An institution cannot serve the Word of God,
     so skeptics have been quick to say,
     and not without a certain right.
     Institutions, since the dawn of civic time,
     be they led by a king, or a priest, or a democrat,
     have served themselves more than not.
     Comedic, then, are all those
          coped and mitered prelates,
          those black-gowned pastors,
          and those smiling slick-suited preachers.
     Tragic, then, are the ecclesiastic courts,
          the self-righteous judgments,
          and the silver-lined purses
          stuffed with the widow's mite.
     All are destructive.
          No, downright deadly.

So why should it be supposed that anyone can beat those odds?
     Institutions shall ever serve their own interests, not God's.
     Should not you Christians know that better than any other?
     For was not your Jesus
          arrested by priests of the most venerable line?
          judged by the most righteous and learned scholars?
          executed by the governors of that empire renowned for its rule of law?
     Are we not right to say that you were quick to build your own order,
          borrowing elders from the ancient synagogue,
          overseers from the holy Essenes,
          and priests from the celebrated temple?
          Did you not transmute them into your own sacerdotes?
          And as any human community fearing death,
          did they not choose to use death to fend off death?

Yes, that is the unholy truth. But not the whole truth.
     These stains have indeed washed over and compromised
     something more original
     and therefore more perennial
     that did not fear death
     and that would not use death.

Something that came to be
because someone went down
to the place not visited and
from which there is no return—
something that had not yet been experienced,
on which hung a new order,
and it and it alone
born in night,
in nothing more than a moment,
with neither a beginning nor an ending,
yielded an uncomfortable order,
a troubling authority,
but the only one that was at last free from the fear of death
and the addiction of dealing in death.

APHORISM §40 FREEDOM

—◆—

The great unfreedom of modernity seems to coincide with the decline in the freedom of faith. The law made me see what it was to be free, but it was faith that made me free.

APHORISM §41 SONSHIP AND FREEDOM

—◆—

Any time someone cries out John 3:16, "So that everyone who believe in him may not perish, but have eternal life," one should cry back John 8:32: "The Truth shall set you free."

APHORISM §42 FREE WILL

The existence of free will does not need to be proven. It is simply a fact of human experience. What does need to be explained is what free will means. This has been curiously ill served by heated arguments of the past as to whether or not free will exists, including the backhanded claims of various religious orthodoxies that it does but that it has in fact been undone by sin.

The path to understanding the meaning of free will lies in tracing its emergence in human experience. In the reality that underlay its emergence are two things of note: the existence of randomness and the presence of information in things. Randomness is not the foundation of reality, but it is a potential within it. The notable example is Brownian movement, that random moment of very small particles in fluid. The second thing is information in things. The protein molecules of RNA and DNA are well known for their ability to carry information, and should not be considered anomalies, for the simplest ultrasmall parcel of reality carries a line of information in it. These two aspects of reality come together in the firing of axons in the brain. The receptor of an axon compiles chemical signals that are subject to Brownian movement, hence randomness, and accrues information that is set over against the body of criteria. The match of the accrued information with the criteria determines when and how the axon will fire.

This indeterminacy is not free will, but it is the possibility of free will. Free will arrives when the information in things is held as information about the information in things. The essential mapping is done in a memory subject to willful retrieval. The search for freedom lies largely in the enhancement of memory.

AS GOD WILLS

It is God's will that I choose.
  I would like God to tell me
    if I should go to the right or the left.
    If God did, then I would not have to choose,
    which is not God's will for me.

  I would prefer to go to the right, right-wise,
    but right-wise might put my life in jeopardy.
    Then I would choose to go to the left, contrary-wise,
    but contrary-wise might make my life irrelevant.
  So I shall choose, which is God's will for me,
    and if I prosper and live, I shall be a communion for God,
    and if I diminish and die, God will be a communion for me.
As God wills.

APHORISM §43 REASON AND WILL

When reason entertains the idea of free will, it makes itself dependent on a story, for if it allows that something is this, not that, because someone made it so, then there must be a story to which it must attend.

Some would say that to do so would be the end of reason, but that is surely wrong, for reason is enhanced by humility.

It has been said that before men learned this, angels debated this very thing, and it was reported by the apostle Peter that in regard to Christ's suffering, the angels longed to look on it. Though perhaps not all. Wasn't it the pride of the rebellious angels that would not wait for the story?

I KNOW. I KNOW.

The first act of the will is to say, "I know. I know."

To which knowing replied, "I love the will."

Upon which will repeats again, "I know. I know."

APHORISM §44 REASON AND CALCULATION

If reason did not originate with an act of free will, then it is not reason; it could be nothing more than a calculation of sorts.

APHORISM §45 JESUS AND FREE WILL

It is difficult to make a beginning of this exploration because my readers are likely divided between humanists, among whom I would count myself, for whom the beginning lies with the man growing up in the world, and believers, among whom I would also number myself, for whom the beginning lies with God coming into the world. The only solution is to do both and, in the end, to see whether and how they might come to the same conclusion.

Our first beginning is with the boy growing up in Nazareth. The physical-cultural reality of his context determines the vast portion of his experience, as it would for any human. Could it be elsewise without making him in- or unhuman? As a human, he would also be a conscious being. Consciousness is the result of the first act of willing. The act of consciousness therefore establishes that Jesus was not only in the experience but also outside it, producing that strange human quandary that asks, Is this real or not?

While consciousness is an attribute of every human life, it is not developed to the same degree and even varies over time within a particular individual's life experience. The rise of consciousness might be prompted by messages. My father, who was born in a farmhouse high in the Vermont hills, used to say that his mother told him that he was born under a red veil. It signified, she told him, that he would do unusual things, which he indeed did. The Nazarene may well have been told by his mother of an unusual birth signifying a special destiny. Yet it is clear that Jesus stepped out of his family's determination—found in the temple doing his Father's business, rebuffed it; at the request to be seen, he dodged it with the question "Who is my mother, and who are my brothers?" and later he explained, "Whoever loves father and mother more than me is not worthy of me!" As he stepped out and away from his family's determination, so he voided the determination of his village and his nation to define him. Clearly this human Jesus had free will to no small degree.

Our second beginning is with divine will coming into the world in order to save it. It should be confessed that attributing will to the divine is based not on knowledge but on an analogy of faith. From the human will, we intuit a divine will that must be the result of an act that gives rises to a divine consciousness. Coming into the determinant world, which is partly determined because that is its nature and partly determined by a will within it that seeks to reduce, if not eliminate, any indeterminacy that remains for it, a divine will precludes that. The deadly determination of the world cannot be prevented by a so-called divine plan, for any plan would necessarily reduce, if not eliminate, indeterminacy. Necessarily, the divine will wills a will to exist that is superbly free, for only such a will could stop natural and hypernatural determinations from foreclosing the future of the world! If, as believers often do, we raise the question whether Jesus could have chosen not to die on the cross, we must answer that with the affirmative. Otherwise the choice to die on the cross would have no value as a saving act.

Clearly the will of the incarnate one, the Lord Jesus, must be superbly free. This, remember, is the same conclusion we came to regarding the human Jesus. So whichever way you work it, Jesus processed free will—indeed, he must be the freest of all men to have ever lived!

THE END OF THE NARRATIVE: RESURRECTION

APHORISM §46 NARRATIVE AND RESURRECTION

Narrative encounters the idea of resurrection as a conundrum with which it would rather not deal. Narratives deal with events of clear durations and specific locations: a before and an after, a here and a there. The here is conditioned by a there from whence one has come and a hither to which one will go. Without these markers, a narrative becomes a myth.

Resurrection events are reported to be events whose duration is indeterminate, having no before or after, and whose location is undefined, having no there from whence or a hither to which, which supply a narrative with flow. Ouch!

This explains why the occurrence of the ideas of a resurrection is quite restricted, as opposed to ideas about life after death, which are largely universal. Resurrection appears largely in the tripartite tradition of Jews, Christians, and Muslims. Even there, the earliest references to resurrection are found in the later levels of the Hebrew text: Isaiah, Daniel, and Maccabees. The first clear reference, according to the highly regarded Old Testament scholar Brevard S. Childs, is Isaiah 26:19: "May your dead live, my corpse, may it rise." Resurrection is, of course, well attested in the later writings of Pharisaic proto-rabbinic Judaism, Paul, and the Gospels. But any serious student of the Gospels knows that the resurrection narratives are fragmented and absent, as in Mark, or relatively brief. It is generally argued that the Gospel tradition began with a passion narrative. Birth narratives, healing narratives, and teaching narratives arose in time to complement the passion narrative, but they are never quite as impressive as the passion narratives. Anything like a resurrection narrative is later yet and even more constrained.

This leads to the conclusion that the resurrection is not subject to narration and that it sits with the narrative tradition as an end or as an intersection. As with an end, an intersection can happen only once. In relationship to a narrative line, it is a single point that cannot be replicated and can only be reprised by means of memory. This leads to the uncomfortable dependence on others for those who choose to believe in them.

That is not, however, to say that resurrection is irrelevant to narration. Would there have been a passion narrative if the idea of resurrection had not occurred?

To take that a step farther, would the vast body of Western narration have happened had a resurrection claim not been made? At first look, this will appear to be an unsupported exaggeration on my part! What is the alternative? Suppose one were to take off from the homeric tradition and extrapolate a path from it to Don Quixote *or* Hamlet—*will one get there? Recall that when the poet came to the court of Augustus to inaugurate a new age with a poetic masterpiece, the result was not a narrative but the reprise of a myth. So just when would you propose that the transition from myth to narration came about if it is not tied to the resurrection of Jesus of Nazareth?*

IN TIME-SPACE

If you told me that God had appeared in a certain place,
　　I would hearten and would ponder making the trip.
　　After all, humans are forever undertaking pilgrimages
　　to the ends of the earth, to the hidden navel, or to the gate in the desert.
　　But if you tell me that God had appeared at certain time,
　　I would be put off. Why would God appear at a point to which I cannot go
　　except by depending on others through a chain of remembering?

The truth, however, is that nothing God has done
　　has happened in time-space alone and there is no going
　　to anything that is real or eternal except through the other.

AN INTERSECTION

On the road of dejection
　　　came an intersection
　　　not from before
　　　and not from behind
　　　but from out of time.

　　　In it stood the other,
　　　and the talk that started gentle
　　　began in time to shatter the shell
　　　in which the ancient writings,
　　　the law, and the prophets
　　　had for so long been left to dwell.

　　　First it cracked, and then it fell,
　　　exposing a wounded savior,
　　　warming the frozen hearts
　　　of the two walking that road.

　　　And, oh, how their hearts did burn,
　　　but their feet grew weary
　　　and their bellies empty
　　　with the passing day.
　　　So they stopped for bread
　　　and invited the other in
　　　to be their companion.
　　　When the crust broke
　　　and fell, the other was gone,
　　　revealing a wounded savior.

And it was suddenly quite clear that the intersection
　　　had been nothing less than a resurrection
　　　not from before and not from behind
　　　but from out of time.

APHORISM §47 RESURRECTION AND LOCATION

———— ⊰◈⊱ ————

If the relationship between resurrection and narrative is problematic because it is not an event in time, it is further problematic in regard to location. At least for some, the larger problem for imagining a resurrection is the limits of space, not time. The question about space is related to the question of body, since the function of a body is to establish location by occupying it. The risen body, however, is an odd placeholder, being both there and not there, much like a resurrection event is then and not then.

Any answer to the question of location requires us to undertake the task of imagining a body that has the capacity of being a placeholder for a particular moment, without being bound to a location in time-space.

APHORISM §48 WITH WHAT BODY?

Our general experience is that bodies can be in one and only one place, which implies that the accounts of the risen body are not credible, unless it is a kind of body that stands outside our general experience. This objection was raised among the Corinthian followers of St. Paul a long time ago. He responded to their objection by posing to them a question: "With what kind of body do they come?" (1 Corinthians 15:35). Paul goes on to answer his question with a metaphor. A seed, a bare kernel, is sown, and what comes forth is the whole plant. More than just a metaphor, his reply takes on the nature of an analogy. The seed is to the plant, what the physical body is the spiritual body, that is, to the body of the resurrection.

Given the science of Paul's time, the discontinuity between a seed and its plant was unbridgeable and could only be dealt with by recourse to divine will. The nature of the plant is assigned by God to a certain seed, just as a spiritual body will be assigned to a physical body. Contemporary science does not invalidate this analogy and may in fact make it more interesting. In our science, we understand that the seed is chock-full of information held in protein strings, which will, when activated by the environment, express itself in a developed plant. The physical body, called wetware in some circles, is chock-full of information as well.

In this age of the COVID-19 pandemic, we have learned that the small package of protein that makes up the virus is no fewer than thirty thousand words made up of the letters A, C, G, and U. Invading a cell, it deploys no fewer than sixteen protein tools—taggers, cutters, bubble makers, scissors, copiers, and so on—each of which has an embedded story of its own. Overall, the virus and its sixteen tools must have an information structure that holds them together! If we move from the virus to the human genome, the scale is now two billion words made up of letters A, T, C, and G. Following our observation of a virus, we need to account for the overarching story line of a human body. This flight of imagination allows us to imagine that the human body is not a mechanism but an information system, and to make a beginning in an understanding that "a story" that existed in a physical body confined to time and space could be moved into alternative dimensions beyond time and space. Without joint, ligament, or wetware, the story could exist and could continue to unfold.

The body of glory is a vast and intricate store of information held in an incipient manner in a physical body but fully realized in the spiritual body that will be given to it.

THE BODY OF GLORY

The glory of the heavenly is one thing and that of the earthly is another.
—1 Corinthians 15

I

The glorious body of our Savior,
    the one that hung on the tree,
    was but the seed.
The body of glory belonging to the risen one,
    the one that left the tomb behind,
    was true vine indeed.
Into its twining branches
    I have been grafted
    and from death thereby been freed.

II

There is no doubt that body of glory confronted and spoke,
    containing everything he was and had said to them,
    who had known him as not there and there again.
For a season, forty days or so, they
    witnessed a there on its way to everywhere—
    no wonder they could not take hold of him.
We renew ourselves by attending to their witness
    of his being nowhere, call it Good Friday,
    of his being again there, call it Easter.
So we shall better find him everywhere.

If space can be confronted by the body of the resurrection, clearly space cannot contain it. If space retains anything of such a confrontation, it would be experienced as an emptiness, as in the declaration "He is not here."

In contemporary science, origin-of-the-universe stories generally suggest that in the earliest moments of the universe, there were more dimensions than the four dimensions of space-time, as many, by some counts, as seven or eleven in all. At a certain point, they were left behind—one might better say set aside, as that preserves the possibility that they don't cease to exist and, under some circumstance, can yet be accessed.

In ultimate small-particle studies, it is possible to observe an element of indeterminacy, where a particle is there and not there. If such a particle for the smallest measure of time is not there, one must allow that it has stepped into a dimension not in time-space. The maneuver requires some bundle of information to accompany the particle by means of which the particle can find its way back. It is, to be sure, no small step to move from observing a line of code in the smallest particle to a vision of the vast body of information involved in human individual that is the foundation of that person's identity and a record of his or her acquired life experience, but it is not unthinkable. In fact, when we think about ourselves, it is this body of information and not the physical body that constitutes what we recognize as the self. When we think of the other, particularly if the other is one whom we love and cherish, we think primarily of this structure of information, this rich story, as the them.

The Jesus resurrection requires us to further imagine that this vast body of information that constituted his individual existence did step out of space and then, as it were, step back into it so that it could be experienced again for a moment, in confrontation with witnesses—namely, his disciples.

What Thomas doubted was not the possibility of a reappearance of Jesus. An image of him could be conjured up in a number of a ways that would remind one of the time spent with him, but that would change nothing. Thomas ups the ante and says, "Unless I see the marks of the nails in his hand and put my finger in the mark of the nails and my hand in his side, I will not believe." The body would have to preserve, he is asserting, its whole history, including its woundedness, in order for him to believe.

Into what, then, did Thomas extend his hand, and why did it cause him to cry out, "My Lord and my God"?

INDETERMINACY IS AT THE DOOR

The human self is not the result of some determinate process
     but is born of and lives in the grand realm of indeterminacy,
     which remains on the other side of a door
     or outside a window in the mind,
     visited or not visited by the self,
     which is always teetering
          between unself and more self,
          between calculation and thought,
          between autonomy and communion,
     in the face of the determined world
     that is intent on defining it.
It is clear that while being like us in every way,
     and by being tested in every respect as we are,
     the determined world had sought to define him,
     but from the earliest time of his being,
     he tended to the window,
     held open the door,
     so that he never lost his self,
     nor did he yield to calculation,
     nor did he break communion.

When the determinant world decided that he had to die,
     they stripped him of everything

they could lay hands on,
which only caused him to go more deeply inward,
and hence he was simply
> more a self,
> more at thought,
> more in communion.

When then to the world he was dead,
> through the door the world could not shut,
> on the indeterminacy that lay in the cellar of that self,
> he slid through to the opposite face of the things,
> across which his words spun laced light
> pulled out of all his pasts,
> lodging it in the ground
> out of which futures rise.

But more,
> as when a backward current
> will return for a time to its source,
> he stepped back through the door
> for a brief time and stood again
> in their lives, the lives of those
> who had walked with him.

As a result, indeterminacy was planted in history,
> communion was restored,
> calculation was upset,
> self was refound
> in the form of the free self
> sitting at the right hand of the one on the throne.

ON THE METAPHYSICS OF SNARKS

It began in a dream in which I was walking through an art gallery
    and found myself trying to explain to the one who accompanied me
    what he was not seeing, he having voiced his lack of appreciation for abstractionists.
    My defense took the course of arguing that he should try to imagine an artist
    trying to paint a brush moving.

    As soon as the artist had managed to delineate a credible brush, I declared,
    he would have failed!
    He would then need to erase some of his lines,
    or perhaps smudge some of his colors,
    so the brush would begin to disappear,
    allowing his observer to see some kind of movement.

    What happened in the dream was a loop
    of dissolving and defining a brush moving,
    which churned onward ever more darkly,
    until the only resolve was in waking.

Awake, I found myself at first bemused
    and then convinced that I had in the dream
    discovered the metaphysics of snarks!
    "Where but at the edge of a dream could such a thought come?"
    What possible purpose this metaphysic might have
    eluded me for a moment, and then it occurred to me
    that it fit that man
    who had stooped that morning
    to look into the cave and saw nothing
    and at the same time saw everything.
Oh, John!

WHAT MARY SAW

Mary in the garden
    saw something move
    and thought it was the gardener.

    What she saw was one teetering on the edge,
    and she heard it say to her, "Mary, be not afraid."
    To which she replied, "My teacher," and reached out to take hold.
    At which point she was told, "Do not hold on to me,
    because I have not yet ascended to the Father.
    Go tell the brothers that I go before them to Galilee."

    At which point that one slid more deeply around the edge,
    where the stream of meaning grew and flowed out more broadly
    across the counterface of reality but not yet so far as to not come back
    to Peter,
    to the two on the way,
    to eleven in an upper room,
    and to many others, perhaps as many as five hundred.

O Mary of Magdala,
    tell us then—what did you do?
    I went, as I was bid, to tell the disciples
    that the tomb was empty and that I had seen him there.
    They were unimpressed and told me that what I had seen was his image.
    They told me that they all had their own image of him that brought them comfort.
    I told them this could not be right for an image of him I would have recognized
    right off.
    But as it was, I did not recognize him there.
    If it was my image of him, I would have called to him.
    But as it was, I did not call him; he called me.
    It was he.
    Still they doubted me
    and said it could not be.

O Mary, once delivered by him of seven demons,
    tell us then—what did you really see?
    It seemed, she said, somehow as if his body had become a door,

which sung out and was hid, only for a moment to swing in
to be seen by me.
In truth, it was too much to see;
I think that is why at first I failed to recognize him,
for through him I was seeing all he was to me,
          in the time of my possession,
          in my works of provenance,
          in the grand procession,
          in my weeping beneath the cross,
not as a vague recollection in the back of my mind
but as reality in my face.
It was, I must confess, the greatest pain
and at the same time the greatest joy.
You yourselves will see.

FIRST TO PETER

———◆———

Peter had cowered through the Sabbath of shame,
    and when it had released him,
    he fled down the road that led
    toward his home in Galilee.
    Suddenly, to his surprise, he had stopped—
    his body would not move on.
    Puzzled, he charged his body to arise,
    upon which it rose and fell.
    The curse that followed from his lips was worse.
    Yet his body stood only to freeze again.
    "Fool," he had said to his body, "would you have me beat you?"
    "Oh, my Master," it replied, "do you not see
    across the road lies fire and a sword?"
The Master at that point joined his body,
    and Peter cried out, "Is that you, Lord?"
    Then that which was in the road called his name.
    "Peter, was it not by the women told to you
    that I would go before you to Galilee?
    Therefore, rise and return to the upper room
    where I broke bread.
    Join your brothers, and I will appear,
    for no longer am I among the dead."

WHAT THOMAS TOUCHED

About the apostle Thomas's brash demand
      to thrust his hand into the Savior's side
      the Easter narrative would appear to be unclear,
      allowing Thomas to do what Mary was forbid,
      if in fact he actually did—it doesn't say.
      Just as the narrative doesn't attempt to square
      one appearance with another.
      Remember I have forewarned you elsewhere
      that in regard to narrative, resurrection has its limits.
      As to what Thomas would have actually touched,
      it would seem not to be a physical body,
      for then he surely would have wept with grief
      or blushed with shame for not having been there.
      But the narrative simply records that he cried,
      "My Lord and my God,"
      which makes me think he touched
      or was touched by indeterminacy,
      which wrecked his determination
            to believe only what he could see,
      which makes me think he felt
            or was felt by infinity,
      which jarred his orientation
            to make his home in Galilee,
      explaining why he then traveled eastward
            down the crescent to the coast of Malabar
            and was martyred on the mount of Chennai.

APHORISM §50 A HAPAX

In textual studies, words that occur only once are referred to as hapax legomena and are considered troublesome since there is no further context to establish the words' meanings. We can borrow this term to express the status of the resurrection of Jesus.

Something that occurs only once presents science with a problem since the basis of scientific knowledge is dependent on the possibility of repetition. So it is clear that a resurrection is beyond science, but there is no reason to consider it to be contrary to science.

It should be clear that the claim for the resurrection of Jesus is not ad hominem, a reward, and/or a vindication for Jesus, but it is the future of us all. There will not be additional discrete resurrections, as if a resurrection of a discrete individual were possible. The wholeness of an individual entails the presence of others, since the field that constitutes a body arises not because of the polarity within the physical body, a so-called north-south pole, but because of the polarity of the other. It should be evident that with the withdrawal of the other, the field begins to collapse.

The possibility of our own resurrection is contingent on his resurrection and is in a sense, if it happens, a continuation of the original resurrection.

LIGHT OF CHRIST

At the Easter Vigil, Compline's collect thanks God
  for "the light of the resurrection,"
  which sets me to thinking what light that would be.

This thought, of course, would begin with the light
  that was in the beginning, as John's Gospel declares:
  "The light was coming into the world,
  and the world knew it not."

To wit, every mind has been opened by that light,
  which, in the mind, sketches a horizon,
  providing a primal knowledge of God
  even in the mind's unknowing.

That light can in fact be seen
  flashing from the eyes of others
  though it is not a little hid
  behind clouds of calculation.

Then it says, "The light was in the world,
  and the world received it not."
  Jesus's mind was opened by that light
  as with all men, but more than a horizon,
  in his mind, it lit there a dome,
  providing the final way of knowing God
  even behind the clouds of crucifixion.

That light could in fact be seen
  flashing from his eyes
  though others often thought it unwise
  to look on it for fear of where it might take them.

Finally: "The light shines in the darkness,
> and the darkness did not overcome it."
> As the Word kept a silence for a little while
> and then the silence broke.
> So the light dwelt in the darkness of the tomb for a little while,
> and then that light flashed across the universe
> unlike anything since the first day.

So when the body stood again, reordered,
> it was transparent in a way that the interior light
> shown not just through its eyes
> but through its every pore.

APHORISM §51 RESURRECTION AND ULTIMATE JUDGMENT

In the early references to resurrection that occur in Isaiah, Daniel, and Maccabees, the connection of resurrection with the divine judgment is quite clear. In a sense, they are synonymous. Life after death is where the last—that is, the ultimate—judgment takes place. Resurrection results in the return of the unwanted who have been dispatched without justice. No one can stand again unless all stand again, and in that confrontation, justice will be done.

Ultimate justice is often dealt with as a question of theodicy. In its classical form, the question of theodicy is put as a question: Why do bad things happen to good people? The presumption of this formula is that we know who good people are and that the separation between these allegedly good people and the not-so-good people is a distinct line. But in reality, it is not so clear who good people are, and it is a questionable virtue to wish to be so distinctly separated from other people as to have a distinctly different destiny from them. I should like to think that I would prefer to suffer the same destiny as other people than to have a different destiny at the cost of being separated from them. Somehow it occurs to me that the one called Jesus of Nazareth felt the same way.

The question of theodicy is generally treated as problem of creation—namely, early on in the foundation of theological discourse. There it is connected with a discussion of free will. It is general assessment that these attempts are seriously flawed, and the best theologians are apt to agree to their limitations in treating these difficult subjects. In part this failure lies with the locus of the discussion and why in the course of our aphorisms I have reserved to our final considerations. Theodicy is resolved only in resurrection.

DEAR EDITH

On the night before my wife and I were due to visit the Documentation Center in Nuremberg, on the edge of sleep, I drafted the following letter to you:

> My dearest Edith, or should I call you Teresia Benedicta a Cruce. Please allow me to follow you out of the door of your Carmel, like Simon of Cyrene followed our Lord out of the gate of Jerusalem to the place of the cross.

THEODICY AND THE PANDEMIC
2020

Early on, when the rumors reached us of your possible return,
  I responded somewhat abstractly, trying, as it were,
  to get my head about the issues that heralded your arrival.
  I did the science that kept you at a certain distance,
  but at the growing insistence of your approach, I thought,
Good God, is it possible for a twenty-first century American male,
  one who is about to flip his eightieth year,
  to know at last God's wrath?
    Which sounds so medieval!
     Biblical!
      Apocalyptical!
    Yet the latter means "an unveiling of hidden things,"
    which certainly seems to fit the way in which this pandemic
    has come so suddenly upon us.
I am moved to confess that I am beginning to see
  that the Lord's law is indeed a two-edged sword,
  one that cuts both ways.
Look and see—the sword on its outward swing cuts for the good.
  The law of viral RNA had a role in the evolution of eukaryote cells
  that led to the Anthropocene,
      to the *tavel*, as it is called in biblical Hebrew,
      to the abundant life, which we are more likely to call it,
      in which I have been allowed to pass my days.
  So should I not say to my soul, "Soul, you are indeed much blessed,
  as one can plainly see, from the abundance that surrounds you"?
      No, not so! The rain falls on the good and the bad.
      There is nothing personal about this abundance.
      It came to you with no quid pro quo, as they say,
      and your wellness, oh, my soul, comes not from it,
      for you are, as you should well know,
      not saved by the law.

Look again and see that the sword on its backward swing cuts for the bad.
  The law of viral RNA has a role in the diseases of humankind,
  which has led to pandemic, to plague, to wrath, in biblical Hebrew
  and hence to a pandemonium of sickness and death everywhere.

So must I not now say to my soul, "Soul, you are indeed cursed,
as anyone can plainly see, by this pandemic under which you now live"?
No, not so! The rain falls on the good and the bad alike.
There is nothing personal in this wrath under which you live.
It came to you with no quid pro quo, as they say.
Your unease, my soul, comes not from the wrath,
for you are, as you should well know,
not condemned by the law.

So if, my soul, you are defined neither by abundance nor by disease,
then it should be clear to you that your worth
comes from the thoroughly personal and gracious choice
of God for you, from God's free gift of love to you, for you,
as you should well know,
are saved by grace.

So I will define my soul not by abundance or wrath but by love,
for which reason I shall say my God, "I worship you."
Good God!

AT THE END OF ALL THIS

You may have come to the conclusion
      that I have been stumbling about this theme of resurrection,
      and you may feel compelled to ask me
      if I really do believe in the resurrection.
      As to your description, I should reply
          I think it is correct,
          I have been, and I continue to stumble about it.
      And to your question, I should reply
          I confess it daily, as I have for seventy-some years,
          and I expect to do so until the moment that I die.
If I could get my head around resurrection,
      the claim that it intersected our history would be denied.
          As it would be if our history were in fact
          a sequence of blind events or as if it was a creation of our minds.
          In the first case, there is no line for a resurrection to intersect.
          In the second case, there is a line that a resurrection cannot find.
      Which leaves me with the conviction
          that not getting my head around it
          makes it more believable than not.
      For I cannot unthink it without the loss of my—that is, our—history.
      Nor can I rethink it without reducing my—that is, our—history to an idea.
Should I then come to the conclusion
      that I should stop thinking about this resurrection?
      No, I should rather think better of it!
      Even if it means more stumbling about.

APHORISM §52 SILENCE RETURNS

———◆———

No word has ever been issued that did not come from silence, and no word has ever been issued that does not end in silence. I am ready for the silence.

HE IS THE ALL

———◆———

We could say more but could never say enough.
Let the final word be "He is the All" (Ecclesiasticus).

Yielding then to Job's advice,

"If now you would keep silence, that would be your Wisdom" (Job 13:2),

I will.